Blastoff!

To Brad!
Keep blasting off

Copyright © 2014 by Jonathan Gilliam

All Rights Reserved.
Published in the United States by MomoBooks,
a subsidiary of SBDP LLC of Austin, Texas USA.
www.MomoBooksInc.com

MomoBooks and the Momentum Factor, FieldWatch and Reputation Defense logos are trademarks of Momentum Factor and SBDP LLC

MomoBooks are available at special discounts for bulk purchases for sales or promotions or corporate use. Special editions, including ersonalized covers, excerpts of existing books, or books with corporate logos, can be created in large quantities for special needs. For more information, please contact sales at info@momobooksinc.com.

Library of Congress Cataloging-in-Publication Data

Gilliam, Jonathan.

Blastoff! Creating Growth in the Modern Direct Selling Company - Lessons on Momentum from CEO's & Industry Insiders / Jonathan Gilliam.—1st ed.

1. Business & Economics : E-Commerce - Internet Marketing.
2. Business & Economics : Marketing – General
3. Business & Economics : Marketing – Multilevel

ISBN 978-1497482425

Printed in the United States of America

Edited by Al Desetta

Interior Design by Rochelle Mensidor

Cover Art Design by Welly Santoso

10 9 8 7 6 5 4 3 2

Blastoff!

Creating Growth in the Modern Direct Selling Company

Lessons on Momentum from CEO's & Industry Insiders

DEDICATION

To my Dad, Hank who created in me curiosity and a love for writing, and to my Mom, Louise who instilled in me a knack for business and flair for the creative.

And to all four of my amazing girls at home whose love and support are all I really need in life. I love you all to infinity.
Go Gilliams!

CONTENTS

ACKNOWLEDGEMENTS

Many people helped in the making of this book. First a huge THANK YOU to the many executives and experts who graciously and generously contributed their time to this effort. You are a special breed. You not only contributed your invaluable insights and experiences, but some of you even reviewed the manuscript and contributed your own content. The ethos of helpfulness in this industry never ceases to amaze.

To my wife Leanna, thank you (again) for your love, patience and support. You are the *womd*.

Thank you to our amazing clients, many of whom are featured in this book, and special thanks to the Momo team. You are the finest collection of digital experts this industry has known.

Thanks also to my editor Al Desetta who is as kind as he is gifted.

A special thank you to the amazing staff and leadership at the DSA who work tirelessly to improve and protect this industry. Their work likely has a greater impact on each one of us than we will ever know.

Thank you to my friends and to all those who made this book possible, including Mark Adams, Jennifer Anderson, Serena Ayscue, Kody Bateman, Brad Brockbank, BK Boreyko, John Breitbart, Kerry Breitbart, John Breitbart, Richard Brooke, Kerry Brown, Tim Brown, Amy Cadora, Trey Campbell, Peter Cartwright, Richard Cole, Kimberly Cornwell, Kate Donovan,

Sheri Gauthier, Jan Gilmore, John Gustin, Ivy Hall, Rob Hawthorne, Dan Jensen, Trace Jensen, Kevin Larson, Michelle Larter, Sheila Marcello, Frank Mannarino, Abbie McClung, Solomon McCluster, Stuart McMillan, Roger Morgan, Christy Prunier, Brett Redd, Spencer Reese, Steve Richards, Andi Sherwood, Robert Snyder, Jamie Stewart, Preston Stewart, Andy Smith, Terrell Transtrum, Mick Twomey, Ryan Wuerch, Angela Yost, and Anna Zornosa and so many more.

Thanks also to our partners, consultants and suppliers who to trust us to take care of their clients, and the wonderful direct selling professionals and field reps who continue to support our firm.

This really is the best industry in the world, and I'm truly proud to be a part of it.

FOREWORD

Kody Bateman, CEO, SendOutCards

One of the things I know we can now count on these days in the direct selling industry is *change.*

This is a new thing for most of us. We haven't had to really alter what we do for most of our history. We've been doing it the same way for fifty years. Meet, enroll, sell, repeat. The environments and techniques may have changed over that time, but the core model has remained pretty much the same.

Today though, we are experiencing tectonic shifts in our model and how we go to market — tectonic in the sense that they are happening at a fundamental level deep below, and are not always so noticeable up here on the surface.

Even the nature of what a "friend" is has changed. People learn more about your product and opportunity before you even talk to them today. If you introduce someone to a product or opportunity, they can learn everything they need to make a decision in ten minutes with a quick online search, versus the weeks it took only few years ago. How does this apply to our belly-to-belly, face-to-face business?

This immediate availability of information is of great benefit—and risk—for our companies. It leads to greater transparency in what we do and makes us accountable, but it also means our message is not under our control. And a message not under our control can be distorted, twisted and misshapen by external parties who don't have our best interest in mind, and even by our field who do. Not only that, the distorted message can make it to a regulator or go viral to millions, instantly.

It can be a tightrope that many companies inadvertently tumble from, as you can't always control everything independent reps say or do.

I've recently taken the stance that Compliance is our best friend, and we can't afford to be wishy-washy about it. Along with leveraging the technologies to grow our company, we are also using technology to do everything we can to protect the business online, which means ensuring our reputation stays clean and that our field stays compliant. We've hired Jonathan's firm to help do both of those things—if a regulator ever knocks on our door, we can point to the technology and say, with confidence, that we are doing everything in our power to run a tight ship. Momofactor's technology and skills are helping us a lot in that regard.

At the end of the day, your credibility will be your strongest business partner. Being vigilant, transparent and building trust will help you maintain your momentum in this business.

If you asked me ten years ago, "if we built a technology that could network everyone on computers and phones in a completely wild and free environment, would you buy it?" I would have said, "Heck no! I'd rather just stick to what I do best and not enter that crazy world."

Well the crazy world is ours now. We have a choice: We can choose to get steamrolled by it, or we can accept the challenge, learn how leverage it and make it ours. I choose the latter.

At our company, we've been a little bit late adapting to some of these things, even with our product being 100% purchased online. Our entire user experience is online. But we've caught up and are now aggressively exploring how we can make these changes work for us. Not because we thinks it's neat technology or because we like tinkering around, but because we have to. Our goal now is to deploy be leading-edge technologies that will help people share our products and mission.

And guess what? It turns out that it's really exciting. We're having a blast. We get to do what we do best, innovate in new and clever ways. Not only is our internal team pumped up about it, but our field feels the energy and can't wait for what comes next. Isn't that what we all want?

I suggest you read this book all the way through. The knowledge and insight shared here will help every direct selling executive plan, launch, build and sustain momentum, and deal with the continuing shifts that occur in this new world. Do your research, trust your why, and execute on it. When your product, tools, and why resonate with your field, your company will maintain a solid orbit.

The future is ours. *Ready, set – blastoff!*

Kody Bateman
Founder and CEO, SendOutCards
Author, *Promptings®* and *MLM Blueprint®*

PREFACE

This book is written for the people of the global direct selling industry. The passionate company executives (many featured herein) who strive every day to improve people's lives and contribute to the social good, the first-time sales reps excitedly setting up their first parties, the field leaders who inspire so many people to better themselves every day, and the experts and consultants dedicated to bringing the best resources and solutions to bear for their clients.

After completing my last book, I swore off writing another. I wasn't getting any younger or less busy, and doing this takes a lot out of you. During the writing process I even regretted taking it on, but afterward, once I could be proud of the text (which does not come easily) I was really pleased to be able to make a new contribution to this great industry and, in my own little way, help shape its future.

Since *Social Selling* was published two years ago, I have been told many times by industry executives that the book was just the encouragement many of them needed to make a decision to commit the resources necessary to move forward and address the cultural and technological forces that had suddenly changed everything. The industry has since progressed in both its understanding of our connected world and learning how to leverage it. This is a wonderful thing, and has been so fun to watch and be a part of.

As exciting as this is, there's more to be done. In this bigger, more broadly focused book, I hope to challenge once again the idea that we can rest on our laurels and that the future will always be there for us if we just stick to our knitting.

The future is already here, and we better get moving!

Blastoff!

Creating Growth in the Modern Direct Selling Company

Lessons on Momentum from CEOs and Industry Insiders

By Jonathan Gilliam

Author, ***Social Selling: How Direct Selling Companies Can Harness the Power of Connectivity...and Change the World***

Founder & President, Momentum Factor

INTRODUCTION

There's a sweet spot where every direct seller wants to be. It's the moment when your products are just right, your people are fired up, the marketing's on target, and the timing's good. Credibility and trust in the company are high, and social media is creating a buzz. You reach a tipping point where things simply take off, and the company soars and does really well. If you have 10,000 people selling for you and each of them recruits two people a day, you're at 20% growth *per month.*

That's what *Blastoff! Creating Growth in the Modern Direct Selling Company* is about—creating and sustaining that sweet spot when growth takes off. This book offers ideas that will hopefully change your understanding of momentum in direct selling, and provides practical, concrete strategies you can immediately put into action, whether you're the founder of a startup who wants to create growth out of the gate, or an executive at a mature company who seeks to reignite and sustain growth for the long term.

Blastoff! uses the principle of rocketry to explain the basics of direct selling momentum. A successful rocket launch takes many months or even years of careful planning before liftoff. After countdown, a massive amount of energy is required for the rocket to escape friction and gravity and reach orbit. In fact, a rocket expends about 70% of its fuel escaping the atmosphere's drag. Once the countdown ends and its engines ignite, performance must be flawless. One mistake, one miscalculation, and the rocket may veer off course and come crashing to Earth.

Rocketry is an apt analogy for the world of direct selling. We know some companies explode on the launch pad, never achieving liftoff. We also know some who've enjoyed dramatic launches, only to falter, crash, and burn in spectacular fashion before they've escaped the Earth's atmosphere. And then there are the companies that launch perfectly and reach orbit, where they cruise along seemingly without effort, but later struggle to sustain the momentum that got them there.

As a direct selling consultant who has crossed paths with hundreds of companies over the years, I continue to wonder why some companies burn out and disappear forever, while others take off and reach the heavens. *Blastoff! Creating Growth in the Modern Direct Selling Company* seeks to the answer by asking a number of crucial questions: What creates momentum? What best practices do we need to embrace? What growth-killing mistakes and pitfalls must be avoided? How can momentum be sustained? How can we revive it when it begins to languish? And, in a rapidly changing world, how can direct sellers leverage advances in consumer and online technology to fuel growth?

What creates momentum? What best practices do we need to embrace? What growth-killing mistakes and pitfalls must be avoided? How can momentum be sustained?

To find the answers, I interviewed industry experts with decades of experience—founders of companies, CEOs, and consultants who know the industry inside out. Their collective wisdom provides an inside look at "industry stuff"—hard-earned lessons that can help executives and leaders avoid mistakes and become better at what they do. *Blastoff! Creating Growth in the Modern Direct Selling Company* is packed with actionable concepts and concrete examples that can teach everyone in the industry how to make the most of new opportunities.

My last book, *Social Selling: How Direct Selling Companies Can Harness the Power of Connectivity...and Change the World*, explored the need for companies to embrace the revolutionary tools of social media and technology to compete in a new industry era. The book explains how the business has changed, how it has gravitated toward online and virtual relationship-building in the last few years, and how we now inhabit a transformed world full of new avenues to create exciting ways to build companies, and the associated risks of that.

Social media and new technologies are influencing in profound ways the way direct selling is done. This new and sometimes bewildering landscape makes some uncomfortable because they're used to the old ways of doing business. Now, more than ever, we need to take advantage of every tool available to us, as direct selling continues to grow due to a variety of factors.

It's clear that the wind is at our backs. According to the DSA's *Growth & Outlook Survey*, direct selling is projected to see annual growth of up to 5% during the next few years, reaching approximately $38 billion by 2017.

Technological advancements powerfully influence that growth. According to the GfK Roper report *U.S. Consumer Trends Impacting the Direct Selling Industry* (also sponsored by the DSA), technological advancements are one of the top reasons small businesses continue to prosper in the U.S., by lowering the cost of entry for business ownership.

From my interviews with executives and field reps, I found that people in our industry almost universally hunger for modern, forward-looking tools that help them conduct and manage their businesses quickly and on the go. Mobile apps and robust social connectivity are no longer luxuries in our industry. They are necessities.

The message is clear: those companies that integrate technology into every aspect of their business will be the winners in the next generation of direct sellers.

Today, a whole new generation is socially connected. They're completely mobile-enabled and have grown up digital. They're simply not attracted to businesses that aren't technologically savvy. Millions of them have never known a world without personal digital and socially empowering technology. Our industry must engage this generation to be successful.

The message is clear: those companies that integrate technology into every aspect of their business will be the winners in the next generation of direct sellers.

Take a look around. What do you notice in the "hot" direct sales companies today? By and large, these companies embrace technology and social media to help advance their businesses, some even deploying variants on our much vaunted business model.

Look around again. The companies that haven't successfully embraced technology are gradually losing ground, with their executives scratching their heads along the way, trying to figure out why. This is the likely outcome for those who ignore the advances in technology—less shock and awe, more hem and haw, which will eventually put them out of business.

> The likely outcome for those who ignore technology is less shock and awe, more hem and haw.

Indeed, the direct selling industry still isn't fully up to speed on this issue. If you want to blastoff, if you want to grow and sustain momentum, you *must* adapt to these new ways of doing business. This book will help show you the way.

Before the mid-2000's, for nearly a hundred years, the traditional way to build a direct selling business was face-to-face—people met in their homes or coffee shop or hotel conference room to demonstrate a product or discuss an opportunity. One person signed up under the other, and then they met someone else and did the same thing.

Today, they meet in online social groups and forum sites and develop relationships that way. Or they send invitations to a party to their friends via Facebook, rather than calling them, perhaps even hosting their own virtual party in real time.

Conference calls used to serve as a primary way we communicated, one of the few ways we could reach masses of people in real time to keep them motivated and informed. The conference call hasn't gone away, but they're increasingly less effective as fewer young people will set aside the time to participate. Now the industry uses a myriad online technologies and techniques, from websites and blogs, to social media and online ads, to reach people, sign them up, and sell products.

Another staple in the industry has been live events and national conventions—over-the-top motivational and educational rock shows, with thousands of people in an arena cheering on the founder of the company, distributors who've achieved a new rank, and exciting new products. That momentum leads to more events, bringing in ever more people to learn about the company. This has been the lifeblood of the direct selling industry, with the mantra: "Always promote to the next event."

Events continue to serve as an effective tool for recruiting, motivating and retaining the field. But today, some upstart direct selling companies don't even offer in-person events. They are strictly building themselves online. While the debate continues as to whether these online-only companies are "real" direct sellers, one thing is clear — the game is changing.

That's the world we are in—one where the rules have drastically changed and will continue to evolve faster than they ever have before. This has significantly altered and even finished many mainstream industries. Remember travel agents, or record stores? Industries around for decades, and in some cases centuries, and have been rendered irrelevant.

One thing is clear — the game is changing.

For our industry however, this new world presents major opportunity. We can now reach untold numbers of people in ways never before possible. Moreover, they can find us. Rather than deflating our business, in the new world it helps us *scale* it. We now have mass instant communication and collaboration at our fingertips, and we can connect with each other in ways never before possible. We can use it to do what we do best—make people feel important and recognized, and help them improve their lives.

Social media is social. Direct selling? *Social!*

And we still get to hang on to our core values as an industry. How cool is that?

The foundation of our industry has always been the person-to-person relationship. We already know how to make connections, build relationships, and cultivate friends. In a certain sense we invented social commerce. Social media doesn't *substitute* for building relationships; rather, it provides a host of new and exciting ways to connect with people.

The better your company is at leveraging new technologies, the more successful your field will be, which will advance the entire industry.

In the end, to succeed in this business, we need to learn and implement best practices and proven principles, the things that successful companies do again and again. This is a never-ending process and there are few short cuts. We all know that direct selling companies, unlike companies in other industries, can be as fragile as a hothouse flower, susceptible to any bad piece of news or big mistake, in a bet-the-company kind of way. One flaw or negative perception can spread quickly through the field and potentially sink the ship. We have to be pretty much perfect in our execution as even a single disappointment can discourage people from selling for you.

My firm, Momentum Factor, specializes in marketing and social media management (the happy stuff), as well as reputation defense and online compliance monitoring (the scary stuff). We help our clients nurture and grow the hothouse flower and protect it from the many unknowns that can cause it to wither and die. Direct selling companies need to be watered, fertilized, and weeded. They must have the right nutrients and sunlight. They are organisms, unpredictable and finicky.

Direct selling companies need to be watered, fertilized, and weeded. They must have the right nutrients and sunlight. They are organisms, unpredictable and finicky.

I hope this book both improves and challenges the culture of our industry. We can be overly optimistic, self-congratulatory, and afraid to say anything negative or self-critical. It can be politically incorrect to look at our warts or baggage. I have always taken a position in the industry that we can do better, and I've found that people appreciate and respond to that frankness. When we conduct business in the right ways, we prosper, the people we work with prosper, and the industry as a whole prospers.

Blastoff! Creating Growth in the Modern Direct Selling Company points the way to a better direct selling industry. I hope you benefit from its advice.

Jonathan Gilliam
Austin, Texas
June 1, 2014

Author's Note: *This industry uses many different terms and titles. For the purposes of consistency I use "direct selling", "network marketing" "person-to-person" "one-to-one" and "multilevel marketing" and "MLM" interchangeably. I also use "distributor" "consultant" or "rep" to cover field sales representatives, associates, promoters, members and the myriad original names used to indicate the independent sales reps in the field.*

There are also, of course many people whose experiences across this great, diverse industry vary and whose opinions may differ from my own or those from the fine folks featured in this book. I always welcome them and value them highly.

PART ONE

The Launch Phase.

A rocket launch is a dramatic, awe-inspiring sight. When the engines ignite there's billowing smoke, luminous flame, and a tremendous roar, but the rocket doesn't move for quite a while. That's because the spacecraft is locked down and the engines are building up energy and force before they let it go. If they release the grips before the engines have harnessed sufficient thrust, the rocket will have no momentum. In fact, it may fall back to Earth before it clears the launching tower (you'll find stunning examples on YouTube).

We use many of different terms in this industry for the components of company launch—pre-enrollment, pre-launch, launch, soft launch, first-year launch, etc. Our industry is always launching. During the launch phase, companies must have sufficient lift to escape friction and the gravitational forces holding them down. They need tremendous amounts of energy and a lot of buildup. If they run out of fuel and can't reach escape velocity, they're going to come crashing back down to Earth. The unsuccessful launch is the rocket that doesn't even clear the launch pad—there's no passion, no plan, poor execution.

A direct selling launch is like rocketry because you're crunching months of potential growth and wealth into the finite period of a pre-launch. It takes a remarkable amount of work and energy, but the end result, if all goes well, is multiple months of revenue coming in on launch day. And that growth starts compounding because of the viral and duplicative nature of network marketing. Your rocket is off the pad and arcing through the atmosphere, escaping gravity's grip.

It's a beautiful sight to behold.

So we're always doing new things. Always looking for something new and exciting to go to. That's what's different about this industry, that other industries don't have—we're focusing on momentum, energy, anticipation, suspense, and the next thing. It's the lifeblood of what we do.

Let's start the "launch" section by taking a look at the component of launch and best practices that set companies on the trajectory to success.

BUILDING THE LAUNCH PAD

The First Phase of Growth.

Direct selling companies employ a sequence of phases as they start out, grow and mature. Often, the first part is the "pre-launch." This is an industry-specific term that signifies the period of work that goes into building the company prior to its debut. More specifically, it is a marketing term that announces publicly that the company is soon to come in the hopes that people want to learn more about it.

What's great about a pre-launch? It's new, exciting (ideally) and who knows, maybe it leads to the next big thing. Any experienced networker is interested in knowing about new pre-launches, if only to learn potential new competitors and what trends to watch out for. In the old days (and even today) networkers would watch for announcements of new companies in the classified section of *USA Today*. This was actually a primary marketing vehicle for pre-launches prior to the Internet and social media.

Pre-launch is when the company is still getting its software and systems together, still putting together the model of who they are and what they want to be. For marketing purposes, they can be used to build suspense. They may even contain a "pre-enrollment" program centered on creating buzz and gathering contact information of interested potential enrollees, to be reached out to later as the company develops.

In a Pre-launch, the company comes out with something new and the idea is to catch people's attention, build excitement, and blow their minds, with the result that they buy in and the business starts to grow the moment you launch.

Sometimes, a company will deploy a "pre-enrollment" program. A pre-enrollment is a period of time, usually four weeks, when the company might share partial information about a forthcoming product or company, but holds back on the full story, often even on the name or what the product is. To mainstream marketers, this seems counter-intuitive. The primary goal of a pre-enrollment is not name awareness, but to obtain contact information, generate interest from networkers and others in the company's not-yet-launched opportunity, and then continue to market it to them as the company approaches launch date. As they get excited, they enroll and, if all goes well, they sign up on launch day and the company makes money before the first product is even shipped. Accountants love this—cash flow on day one. At least that's how it's supposed to work.

At one of my direct selling companies we set up a pre-enrollment program that counted down to the launch on a dedicated website and social media, which was (at the time) a new and exciting take on an older idea. After some creative marketing messages and videos, people "pre-enrolled" by submitting their contact info and securing their position in the genealogy. We enrolled tens of thousands of people during our one-month pre-enrollment phase and ultimately converted a nice percentage of them to buyers on day one. We were immediately profitable. At that point, all engines were firing and the rocket was escaping gravity.

Very often following the pre-enrollment, the final phase of a pre-launch is marked by a "soft-launch," when the company's systems and ability to enroll people and ship product are up and available; but, officially, the company is in "beta" mode, and so is somewhat shielded from minormistakes and problems. There usually is no big event connected to the soft launch; the company is open for business and building for the big launch day.

The "launch" is a startup's debut, usually centered on a major event and flurry of announcements and activity. Some companies take up to a full year before their official launch, primarily to build a sufficient field (so the main launch event actually has people attending it) and to work out the kinks along the way.

When the company is in pre-launch, it may have a little more room for mistakes or for growing pains. But at launch it really has to be meticulous about everything.

Launch breeds its own anticipation, because the company wants a packed house at the event. Again, it's the anticipation and suspense building that's important, not just "getting things ready."

Another way our industry interprets "launch" involves the many product announcements and unveilings that established and mature companies use these events to maintain the excitement going and to build on an existing product line. We'll discuss those in greater detail later.

When you're in pre-launch, you may have a little more room for mistakes or for growing pains. But at launch you've really got to be tight about everything.

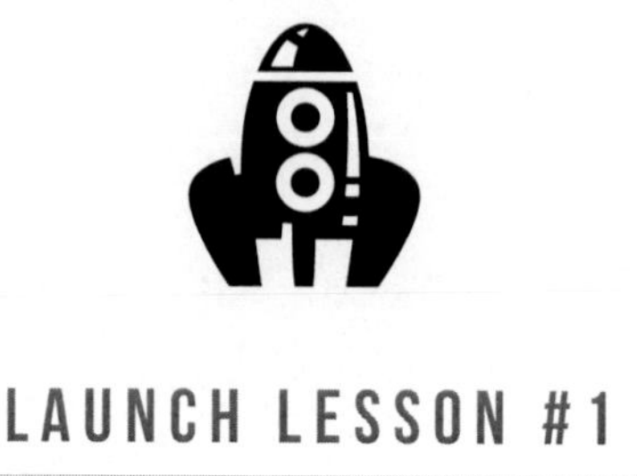

LAUNCH LESSON #1

New to the Industry? Forget Everything You Know.

To those new to direct selling, this industry can be really confusing and not like what they've experienced before. They may have enjoyed success in other businesses, have a Harvard MBA or advanced management skills. But they're often a babe in the woods when entering this business. Direct selling is just a different breed of animal compared with other industries.

If you're a newcomer, the first thing that you should know is that you're no longer in the business of managing people. You're in the business of *motivating* people, and keeping them engaged. If you can't do that, you won't have sales.

They may have enjoyed success in other businesses, have a Harvard MBA or advanced management skills. But they're often a babe in the woods when entering this business.

Why? Because unlike most traditional businesses, which rely on a sufficient level of certainty, pre-determined outcomes and salaried employees, direct selling relies on *people*. And people, as we all know, are not always predictable.

I'll use a metaphor to illustrate. In the commercial world, you buy the facility, get the machinery, and hire employees to do the work. You bring in some MBAs and tweak the financials, make some adjustments here and there, and if everything goes in your favor, the business grows.

In direct selling, you're not building machines. You're planting seeds. And seeds may or may not sprout. They have to be nurtured with water and fertilizer. When they do sprout, the plants may have a single leaf on one branch, and many leaves on another. They may grow in an odd direction, or much faster or slower than expected. Some of them may require an inordinate amount of attention, while others just sprout and grow like mad.

Direct sellers are organisms, literally and figuratively. They're not machines. For people accustomed to building and running *things*, it can be a difficult concept to understand—direct selling is made up of, and completely dependent on, people. Newcomers who don't take this into account or attempt to learn the difference required for managing this business can get in over their heads.

Of course, there are all the traditional challenges of running a business, but the dependence on thousands of independent salespeople adds a critical and often daunting twist. Imagine that in your mainstream business that you have thousands of salespeople working for you. Most mainstream executives shudder at the thought. In a previous career I had five salespeople working for me and I thought *that* was nuts.

> Direct selling is made up of, and completely dependent on, people. Newcomers who don't take this into account or attempt to learn the difference required for managing this business can get in over their heads

Because this industry is so different, it requires managers and experts with direct selling experience in both corporate and the field to really succeed. Sure, many people have come into the industry fresh and later become successful, but even the ones who made it look easy can show you the many scars and war wounds they gathered along the way.

LAUNCH LESSON #2

The Field Are Volunteers, Not Employees.

Another potential pitfall in direct selling is the idea that one can simply identify a product, find a leader, and bring in a whole bunch of people to sell it. Naïve executives often underestimate how difficult it can be to get the field to do what needs to be done to grow the business.

Kevin Larson, VP of Sales for New Earth, emphasizes this point. "One of the biggest mistakes any executive in direct selling can make is to believe that your partner distributors work for you or that you can even control their efforts. This is like playing with nuclear waste; it begins killing you before you even know it. Part of the reason they like this business is the personal freedom it provides. Challenge it at your peril."

This is often a difficult concept for new entrants from other industries to understand. They come from places where they told employees what to do, and the employees did it. They wonder: *Why can't we just make them do it? We're paying them huge commissions!*

The reason is, legally and in all practicality, they don't work for you. They work for themselves. Your primary operational role as a corporate executive is to see that they are paid accurately and that their product arrives on time. Your primary sales role is keeping people excited and motivated, or, as I like to say, "Keeping them from sitting on the couch and watching *American Idol.*"

What keeps people selling for you? Increasing commissions? Sure, but the fact is that this industry is driven by far more than just commissions. The allure of direct selling is the independence it provides (among many other things.)

Successful companies keep wind in the sails of motivation. When their people start to fall off and lose motivation, as sometimes happens, they discover new ways to get them excited again. They know how to leverage new products or a special event to fire up the community. They seek out new ways to reach people where they are and speak to them in ways they prefer.

Successful industry executives understand that their role is not to squeeze more profitability out of people and machines, but to *reward people for desirable behaviors.*

The lifeblood of direct selling is getting people excited and motivated, or, as I like to say, "Keeping them from sitting on the couch and watching American Idol."

LAUNCH LESSON #3

As You Launch, Seek Out the Best Minds.

To minimize the headaches and gotchas of starting a direct selling company, hire the absolute best consultants you can find. The industry is fortunate to feature a robust collection of deeply experienced advisors in every facet of the business, from legal and comp planning, to warehousing and fulfillment, to *(ahem)* social media and marketing. For any challenge you encounter, there is someone available to guide you.

Entrepreneurs attempting to launch a direct selling company don't know what they don't know. And if they are reaching out for help when they're about to pull the launch trigger, it may be too late. (Hint: it is.)

"I've never had an experience where a client new to the business already knows everything that we teach," says Dan Jensen, the industry's leading compensation specialist. "In fact, on average, they know at best about 10% of it. Therefore, reaching out for help is part of mitigating the risk of failure and maximizing the opportunity of success. If they get the right help, they're much less likely to fail."

Don't do this on your own. Reach out for experts well before who have been many times down the path you're now walking.

LAUNCH LESSON #4

Do Your Homework When Hiring Experts.

As you seek help, do your research, and be especially vigilant about whom you hire to guide you. Industry veterans will agree that direct selling has the good kind of experts, but it also has its share of mediocre consultants, software firms and advisors, who provide largely ineffective advice, often steering them to unnecessary programs and wasteful fees.

Do your research on anyone you partner with, look into their reputation, visit as many events and conferences as you can, and ask, ask, ask.

I call it "running the gauntlet": by the time they've found the good guys, the not-so-good guys have already bled them dry. Do your research on anyone you partner with, look into their reputation, visit as many events and conferences as you can, and ask, ask, ask.

One of the better resources for startup advice is the Direct Selling Symposium, an intensive 2-day "boot camp" educational conference held in Salt Lake City each spring and fall. *(Disclosure: we are a founding member).* The Direct Selling Association also offers a great seminar in December called *Smart Start,* part of their annual BeConnected conference.

LAUNCH LESSON #5

Know Their "Why"—And Yours.

People join direct selling companies for various reasons. Some like the community and the recognition or feeling a part of something bigger than themselves. Or they love the product and want to make money selling it. Or they want a second income to pay for their children's education or a special vacation. They're enthusiastic about working hard and motivated to build their own businesses.

That's what is known in the industry as the "why." The *why* is what gets people to join, to stick to it, and to achieve their goals.

The first "why" starts with the company founders.

A lot of questions that will have to be answered in the early days of starting a company, and many foundational principles and issues to consider. One of the most important is *Why are we doing this?* We have to know the "why," both our own and the field's, to be successful, because it will be the underlying driver over the long term.

Terrell Transtrum of ServiceQuest has been a consultant to the direct selling industry for many years. He succinctly summarizes the importance of a company's "why":

"The touchstone of all success in direct selling is when people discover the 'why' behind the company, its products, and its founders. When people discover it, they make the decision to be involved, and we have our best chance at keeping them engaged if we are true to our 'why.' It's a reflection of the way we help people and take care of them and serve them. If there's an alignment between who we appear to be and who we really are, that fuels momentum more than anything else."

What is your company's "why"? The home office must be clear about it, because it will transfer to the field; they're going to pick up on the company's "why." If the executives or founders are in it just to make money, that will become the field's "why" and ultimately unsuccessful, as it isn't enough to sustain a great company. Money, in this case, will become the standard by which you are judged, and soon enough the field moves to the next company promising higher commissions.

But if your "why" is to help people's lives with a great product, that will translate through to your field. When they introduce new people to the opportunity, they'll convey a much more powerful message: *this product will improve your life; this company will help you do great things.* And they'll stay with you because you're meeting more of their needs than just the financial.

Case Study: Saving Lives is a Pretty Good "Why."

A startup direct selling company I recently advised markets electronic cigarettes. They've sold them for several years online via affiliate programs, and it worked well for them. In the affiliate world, all anyone cares about is selling product and making money on it, in volume. In direct selling, there's much more to consider.

I asked the CEO for his elevator pitch, his primary recruiting message, and it went something like this: "This business is exploding! You are going to make so much (expletive deleted) money you'll freak out!"

So, I asked the him why he got into selling e-cigarettes. He told me it was because he knew several people close to him who had died from smoking the real kind. He researched the vapor products and concluded they were a safe alternative to cigarettes. That was his "why."

Now that's a great story! His product can literally save people's lives. Not many companies can claim that, right? I told him that this story is something the field will completely love and it will resonate with them, because guess what? Many of them have had the same experience with their own loved ones. This will carry them much farther than any money story ever will.

Rob Snyder, CEO of Stream Energy, believes the "why" emanates from the real reason the business is started in the first place, and that can't be manufactured or faked. He says too many networking firms are launching without a good "why" into an already crowded marketplace.

"Many don't have a good reason for their existence other than the fact that someone wanted to start up a business," he tells me.

"There has to be a raison d'etre and, on top of that, the value proposition has to be clear and seen as truly valuable to the consumer. The more attractive and valuable it is to the consumer, the better chance you will have of accelerating."

LAUNCH LESSON #6

Know What Makes You Unique.

Dan Jensen approaches companies assertively through queries. The first question he asks is, "If you ran into me on the street, what would you tell me about your products and your company?" It's what we call the *pitch* or the *elevator pitch*: a very important yet often ignored concept.

"When I asked a recent client to give me their pitch, they gave me a high level explanation that was less than compelling, really had no appeal whatsoever," Dan tells me. "Which caused me to ask another question: 'Why would I buy your products instead of walking into a health food store and buying what's on the shelf?' And they said, 'We don't have an answer for that yet.' This is a problem for a new company."

A startup in any industry must have a unique selling proposition. In direct selling, the USP is an essential part of the launch pad. What makes one rocket different from others? Why should someone take a ride on yours and not another? Without a compelling answer to these questions, there's no business.

Jan Gilmore, a well-regarded expert on party plans, dives deep when she works with startups.

"They need to really understand what they've got. I ask, 'Why do you want to do this?' You don't do direct selling because it sounds like a good idea. There has to be a better reason, a reason that will resonate.

"If you have a product with a good a story, if you can touch it, taste it, feel it, try it on, then the party plan is a smart way to work. Instead of having to tell the story ten times, you tell it once to ten people. Plus you get peer pressure to work for you. If you're selling jewelry, someone at the party will say, 'Oh, that looks great on you, you should get that.' And most likely she will, because she trusts her friend more than a salesperson."

Jan also asks startups, "What's your story?" In direct selling, it's the story that drives momentum. Distributors need to be able to tell a compelling story.

Without a story, it's far more difficult to create both the initial interest *and* the motivation for the field to keep going in their businesses.

LAUNCH LESSON #7

Storytelling: An Emotional Connection.

We need to tell stories because the field has to tell a story. It's the story told by distributors that drives momentum. Arming them with the right one is crucial. It needs to be simple, memorable, and easy to tell.

Simplicity is important—simplicity in the product, simplicity in the story, and simplicity in the compensation plan. The field has to be able to digest and cogently tell your story, share your comp plan, and make their business easily understood.

Organo Gold, for example, has a very simple pitch. Do you drink coffee? *Yes*. How much do you spend on Starbucks a day? *About $4.* What if you could spend fifty cents a day buying coffee, and get other people to replace their coffee with healthier coffee and actually make money on it? The story is very simple and easy to understand. It doesn't require knowing the product, science or comp plan.

Our industry has told compelling stories for a century. Stories are the essence of our being and one of the fundmental keys to our success. Few other industries live and die on storytelling like ours does.

In the past, a common theme for network marketing stories laid on thick the fear and doubt. The classic is the video (tapes back in the day) showing a polluted world with smokestacks billowing and water being contaminated. The pitch was that you can have a product that is pure and good for your health that counters all the pollutants and poisons everywhere.

Later the story shifted to focus much more on personal development and improvement, where rags to riches stories ruled the day. "You can do it, too" was the message.

The modern direct selling story may include elements of these, but today the better ones tend to communicate the importance of community, connection and social good, qualities that reflect modern sensibilities and, most importantly, the mindset of a newer generation.

Today, successful marketers have adapted to keep up with what's important to Millennials. It's more about helping individuals becoming better people and presenting them with opportunities for personal freedom and experiences.

It's still focused on the classic WIIFM, or What's In It For Me? It's just that WIIFM has changed from "make me money" to "make me important" and "make me entertained," or maybe "make me adventurous."

Of course, Millennials still need money to be important, entertained, and adventurous. It's just that the message is different.

In addition to the company story, a good *product* story is also essential. What makes for a good product story? I call it "unique plus mystique."

Direct selling products do best when enveloped in a compelling story. It's one of the reasons a product that could never compete on a retail shelf can do wonders in a person-to-person model.

In my hometown of Austin, Texas, SOZO offers products with a special ingredient called "coffeeberry." The coffeeberry is the natural shell that surrounds the coffee bean until it is harvested. According to research, the shell contains amazingly beneficial nutritional properties. During the coffee picking process, the shell is usually discarded as it quickly goes rancid after the beans are picked. So to grab the nutritional content of the coffeeberry, SOZO developed a process that extracts nutrients from the shell and adds those nutrients to their products. People swear by it, there are the clinical studies, and it's a really cool story.

Could coffeeberry sell on a shelf? Maybe. Recently I ran across a SOZO product competitor in a convenience store that featured coffeeberry as a main ingredient. I noticed it only because I know the coffeeberry story, but when I looked at all the other drinks competing for my attention I thought, *there's no way I would have bought this otherwise.* The story just gets lost in a "give it to me fast 'cause I gotta go" environment.

Win: Direct selling.

In Bend, Oregon, a 30-year old company called New Earth (formerly CellTech and Simplexity Health) has a similarly wonderful story about its products. Its primary ingredient, wild blue-green algae, is grown naturally in the waters of a pristine lake fed by an ancient volcano and mountain springs, and carries with it exceptional nutritional properties. The story centers on this natural "Earth's first food," and clinical studies proving its efficacy, appealing to a burgeoning new societal consciousness about what we put in our bodies. They have since complemented the line with other all-natural food-based supplements, such as beneficial mushrooms, all of which align with that same 30-year old story.

If you don't have a story, you're just another product. In our industry, products need a good story or they won't be able to compete. If you don't have a compelling story, what are you going to tell someone? That you have a great energy drink? There has to be more to it than that. And it takes people to tell stories.

Likewise, your company needs a good story that exemplifies amplifies its core principles. Scentsy's story is a great example. Orville Thompson started out making candles on his farm with his kids. That's their message: we started from nothing, for four years we had nothing, and then after four years we had $600 million. His is a classic story of sticking with it. Orville talks about focusing on the reps and not getting too far ahead of yourself, and sticking with things through thick and thin. When people join Scentsy, they feel like they're a part of something important because of that story. They believe they've joined something bigger than themselves. The Scentsy story contributes enormously to the company's success.

In direct selling there's the direct person-to-person sharing—you want to buy something because of the great story I just told you. The story sells the product, and that's how the industry works.

Beyond being easy to share and explain, the story has to make an emotional connection. The emotional connection often comes from the "me"—let me tell you my story, how I found this product, or how this special product changed my life or the lives of my friends.

Every successful company has something like that—a story, a hook. It can be about empowerment, personal development, or just having fun. This company helped me change my life—it made me better, skinnier, and richer. Hey, if I can do it, you can do it too, if you stick with it.

Your story should developed during pre-launch. In this way, pre-launch is like writing a movie script. What makes the product different from other competing products out there? If it's a first-to-market product, what are its advantages? What will it do for people? What's the hook behind it? How is it different or compelling?

Case Study: Xango: Building Trust Through Storytelling

Xango, one of the first superfruit juice companies in direct selling, had one of the most compelling stories in the industry when they launched. They did a great job of describing how they found this seemingly magical fruit on top of a mountain on an island. It was captivating and really drew people in. They did a great job with their video, making the product very exclusive: you cannot find this anywhere else in the world. They explained the history behind it and they backed it up with science.

They also intertwined the story of the product with the story of the founders. It was brilliant, because they hit on all the pieces that needed to be in place to build their credibility. They answered the biggest question that potential joiners are always asking in the back of their minds: *can I trust these guys?* Can I not only trust what they're saying about their products, but can I also trust that they're going to pay me? Can I trust that they're going to be around tomorrow? Can I trust that what they're telling me is true?

Rob Hawthorne, founder of Launch Red and an experienced leader in the field, says that building trust is absolutely critical during pre-launch because you only have that one shot, that one time, when someone brand new is going to learn about your company: "You have to be able to answer their questions immediately: what's the story behind the product, the company, and the founders."

Trust is not going happen in one video. It is built over time, throughout pre-launch and then after the launch. It's ongoing, because you always have new people coming into the business. Trust can be built through webinars, conference calls, in social media, press hits, and videos directly from founders telling the story. All this media can explain why the founders and leaders are so passionate, building their credibility about why they're the right people to be running the company and bringing the products to market.

As important as the story is, it certainly takes more than that to launch a successful direct sales company.

LAUNCH LESSON #8

Why Stop at Just One Story?

As hard as it may seem to develop that one great story, it's important to have even more than one, especially if you're a party plan company. A party with just one story or product is a bit boring, right? And parties shouldn't just be about selling. They should be educational, community-oriented, and group inspiring.

Party plan expert Jan Gilmore stresses the importance of edu-tainment through multiple stories.

"If I come to a party and you show me a single product, I don't need to see it again. I know what it is and I just bought one. What's the hook to get me to come back? For party plans, you need a range of products that lend themselves to more than one visitation and more than one story.

"It certainly doesn't hurt to have multiple uses for your core products, which helps not only sales but also leads to more interesting gatherings.

"For example, a client of mine has a lavender farm. Lavender is very relaxing and stress relieving. They've done some test parties and are on their way. Some parties are about relieving stress, some are about relaxation, and some focus on using lavender in cooking. This encourages people to return for more parties, because, in addition to having fun, they're going to learn something new each time."

LAUNCH LESSON #9

Great Distributors Do Not Necessarily Make Great Company Founders.

Entrepreneurs entering the industry shouldn't underestimate how difficult it can be to succeed. They'll need the right specialty skills and the right expertise—the right consultants, the right team, product, story, and all the selling elements to make it work. Many have tried and failed because they didn't to grasp that direct selling is an entirely different world from the commercial business world.

Our industry attracts people who underestimate the business, who think it's easier than traditional businesses. Perhaps it's the (erroneous) perception that not a lot of capital is needed. Or maybe it seems simple to get people to sell your products and not have to go out and impress a wholesaler or chain stores. "Many new entrants are winging it," says consultant Dan Jensen. "That's a common thing. They just don't grasp how to execute."

In the past, distributors who did really well in the field often decided they could start their own direct selling companies. Arguably, they provide a much needed skill in building the field. But more often than not, they were soon humbled because they did not understand and appreciate the complexity of the business. They viewed things only through the glasses they'd worn as field leaders, which covers only one component of a successful company. They often lacked the business management skills required to run a successful direct seller.

As Dan says "Being a successful distributor doesn't mean you'll be a successful business owner. As a distributor, life is comparatively simple. You're in control. You don't have employees. You have a following.

"As an owner, you have employees that you have to control and manage and work with. You have legal issues. Operational challenges. Production and manufacturing. It's an entirely different world."

Leading a direct selling company today requires expert operational and management skills. Marketing and technology in the industry have also changed dramatically. As capital needs have risen and the level of sophistication increased, today fewer and fewer former distributors are entering the business because the price of admission has climbed.

The new wave of direct sellers is now coming from the commercial sector, who view our model as an attractive channel to market their products. More and more investors and companies from outside the industry are entering direct selling.

Some may debate whether this is a good thing. Are we losing what makes us different, what I described in *Social Selling* our "special something?" Or are we maturing and adding more disciplined business practices to what has been traditionally an insular and somewhat parochial industry?

Like it or not, this is where we are headed. I anticipate that the direct selling future will be comprised of mainstream companies starting direct selling divisions, rather than grassroots or homespun companies.

It's already underway. A good example of this is a client of ours, a major cosmetics and skin care provider seeking to launch a direct selling division. With deep pockets, vertical integration, and smart management, they have a real shot at direct selling success. And rather than enter as amateurs, they hired a veteran industry sales VP and the best consultants and advisors to help launch the company.

The idea of field distributors starting and leading companies without significant managerial and financial backing is no longer the norm. I question whether it's even possible in today's competitive market.

LAUNCH LESSON #10

Lead with the Product, Not the Opportunity.

Determining whether you're going to be opportunity focused or product focused is an essential decision during pre-launch. What balance are you going to strike between the two? That very much dictates how you lay the foundation and the inner workings of your business, and how you work with your sales force.

A good example of the limited power of the compensation plan alone is Scentsy, which Dan Jensen says when it started out had originally replicated a comp plan from a company called Southern Living at Home. "Southern Living went through a period of very strong growth and then fell on hard times" he says. "They called me in to fix their comp plan, while Scentsy was experiencing heavy growth. Identical comp plans, different results. It wasn't Scentsy's comp plan that caused their massive growth. It was the product, the story, and the person-to-person relationship.

"The proof is that some of the industry's best successes—Pampered Chef, for which Warren Buffet paid $900 million in 2002, Nu Skin, Amway, Herbalife, and many others—all had sufficient but not stellar comp plans. Their comp plans, which were all different, didn't drive their heydays of growth. If comp plans were the keys to success, it would be very obvious on paper who the winners would be, when that's not the case at all."

Successful companies bring more than just compensation. They get people excited about the product, the community, the fun, the people, and the trips. They are about the belonging, recognition, achieving goals, and personal development. These are important and powerful things that keep the field motivated and make the company successful. It isn't only the money.

Rob Snyder at Stream Energy supports this point. "Some firms launch without a compelling value proposition," he tells me. "They don't have a compelling product offering. Too many network marketing efforts are launched only for the purpose of making money rather than focusing on the product. "I think there's a lot of that in this industry and it's one of the reasons why direct selling has such a negative connotation in the general population. Too many networkers are trying to sell me-too products at inflated prices that they wouldn't buy themselves."

Richard Cole, CEO of new skin care company Viridia, says, "At the end of the day, for us, it's all about the product. And it's either good or it's not. It's either unique or it's not. It's exceptional or it's not. It does what you say it does or it doesn't. So if your product isn't ten times better than the other guy's, you're not going to make it."

Not only is being product-focused a better business practice and more sustainable, it's actually the regulatory direction we're heading in. The industry is facing greater scrutiny across the globe, with initiatives in China, Germany, Italy, as well as the U.S. and other countries.

The U.S. Federal Trade Commission, having been recently pressured by external forces who have their own agendas, has recently taken a hard look at rules concerning selling to customers vs. recruiting for an income opportunity, the debate coming into greater focus with recent investigations into industry-leaders. There's little doubt that certain regulatory issues aren't going away—in particular, whether people would still buy products if they weren't in the opportunity, and whether the focus of companies is to sell products or merely to recruit sellers.

It is incumbent upon all companies to really think this through and be prepared to adjust accordingly. If your incredible money-making opportunity lacks a product people would otherwise pay for, you need to seek an additional one that works, at the very least.

We need to continue to push out the money games and focus, like we have for many years, on developing and innovating great products that can't be found elsewhere—products that people want.

Some of the world's most innovative consumer products are offered by our industry, products you can't easily find on a shelf. Products people swear by, whose benefits they have known personally, for decades. Personal selling is the best way to demonstrate and explain these kinds of great products.

Ivy Hall, co-founder of Initials, Inc. describes the focus her company puts on its products and the "shareable experience" associated with them. She says the field is seeded and supported by the product.

"So many consultants start out as fans of the products. If they don't have a great experience as a customer, they won't have the desire to be a hostess or represent the product. You must have confidence in the product that you're offering, and in the customer's experience of the product, before you can ever have the host or business opportunity discussion."

Is the customer experience just about the product? Or does it go beyond the product? Ivy offers her thoughts.

"When I look at what makes up the experience," she says, "a product is probably 50% or less of it. The rest is good customer service, an engaging party environment, meeting the field's expectations and timelines, the value proposition in terms of what people are getting for their money, and follow-up. I think there's a tremendous opportunity, especially in today's world where so much is done online, to really exceed expectations of personal service."

When companies focus too much on the opportunity, they tend to attract a disloyal and unfocused group of participants. The money is always greener elsewhere.

Ivy says, "Our mission has never been totally about the money; it's been about what people can do with that money to create opportunities for themselves. For some, it's the additional income that they earn; for others, it's a flexible schedule or an opportunity for travel. Some women use their money to support adopting children or to pay for college. We try not to keep the focus on the money, but on what it can add to people's lives."

Dan Jensen says, "You don't want to create a culture that is only opportunity driven. You want to create a culture that is intense, passionate, and loyal to the product and company first. Connection to and communication of the mission is vital.

LAUNCH LESSON #11

Integrity at the Core.

Integrity is an oft-used term in this industry. Everyone (those with and without integrity) claims integrity is the center of their companies. They recognize that trust and shared purpose are the first, and possibly most important, quality needed for people to join.

Integrity then, is as important to the launch phase as the software, the marketing tools, and the product, or even cash. As Kevin Larson, VP Sales at New Earth puts it, "Our industry's medium of exchange is not money; it's trust."

"To maintain a company of integrity," says Ivy Hall of Initials, "you have to *be* a company of integrity; it filters through to your field and customers.

Kerry Breitbart, Co-Founder & CEO of North American Power speaks about misleading comp plans as something that has to change in the industry.

"I think integrity is the biggest issue right now in direct selling. There has to be a genuine effort to reduce the number of 'gotchas' in the comp plans, and perhaps, as a result, a lower bottom line. The industry needs a more genuine approach to providing a great opportunity for the reps. Because even in a perfect world where you do execute on all cylinders, 80% of the people at most companies are still at risk of not succeeding. For me, I want no part of people losing money that, in many cases, they couldn't afford to lose in the first place.

"So I think there has to be more integrity in how we do things. Ultimately, the laws are going to demand it. There's no room for businesses that barely skirt pyramid laws."

On the other hand, fair compensation plans can help create a meritocracy, says Kerry.

"If you do the job, you get the bonus. If you do it well, you get promoted. In the ideal company, there's no mediocrity at the top that keeps good people from rising. There are no character defects who give bonuses to idiots and punish good people. The perfect direct selling industry leads to a perfect meritocracy, far beyond that of corporate America."

Kody Bateman, founder and CEO of SendOutCards, emphasizes the need for greater professionalism in the industry. "I think it's really important that all of us play a part in elevating our profession, from the brand new distributor in a new company to a seasoned executive. Everybody needs to band together to make this profession more professional. And to do that, we must be more professional and always treat what we do in that manner."

LAUNCH LESSON #12

Run a Tight Legal Ship.

A direct seller grapples with many branding and marketing issues during pre-launch that also have legal overtones and ramifications.

Confronted by the vast expanse of the Internet, we have to make sure that that people representing our brand are telling the truth. Not only that, we need to ensure that our representatives aren't saying things that violate the regulations.

Through our policies and in the conference calls, we need to educate the field about the company's compliance limits. We need to make sure that the field protects its own businesses by knowing what to do and what not to do. Why? If somebody goes off on a tangent and mentions the word cancer or gets the attention of the FTC for an income claim, that puts everybody at risk. We can encourage the field to monitor and police itself. We can encourage the field to speak up when the brand is at risk, so the company is aware of the problem.

My good friend Spencer Reese of Grimes & Reese and a preeminent industry attorney, has represented hundreds of companies in the direct selling industry. He recommends considering the legal ramifications specific to your chosen business model.

"Once you figure out who you are and what you want to be, then you can say, 'These are the sets of laws that are going to be most challenging to me. For example, if you're a party plan, you have to be careful to not trip over the business opportunity and franchise laws. The network marketing programs are not so much worried about that, but they are worried about the pyramid and securities laws, which party plans don't worry about so much. How you do business will dictate what laws you have to be most concerned about. You have to be concerned about all of them, but it's a matter of degree."

Compliance has as much to do with the culture you establish during pre-launch, as it does with setting up the right rules. It's great that people talk about the company, but they can also say things they shouldn't say. A company can be shut down based on an errant online comment from one distributor 2,000 miles away. Companies must be vigilant that their people don't say the wrong things about the product, but it happens all the time.

Spencer continues: "You can set up a company to be legally bulletproof, but if you don't enforce your rules and let the sales force run amok, all the internal legal compliance in the world is not going to help you. This comes back to the question of culture, which is a non-legal issue that has huge legal ramifications: what is the culture you build into your sales force? Is it one of compliance, or is it a bunch of cowboys?"

One of the issues I've seen in our compliance monitoring practice at Momentum Factor is the reluctance of some companies to "rock the boat" with the field by enforcing compliance rules. One of our clients recently explained to me that they just couldn't afford to "mess with the field right now" by approaching them with the kind of communications that compliance sometimes requires. "Too negative" was his answer. My position, logically, was that an inquiry letter or legal action would be much more negative than a few emails to maverick reps.

"In law, an ounce of prevention is worth a ton of cure," says Spencer. That means figuring out who you are and then properly setting up your program to address, in advance, measures that will keep you from going down the wrong path with your sales force and the company as a whole.

Of course, what you are selling is central from a marketing and sales perspective, but it also has huge legal ramifications. If you're selling health supplements or skin care lotions that are regulated, there's the potential for the sales force to be making outlandish or unsupportable claims about the product. Not much of an issue if you're selling jewelry.

There are all sorts of product-specific issues that you have to address and get your arms around.

LAUNCH LESSON #13

Know Your Tolerance for Risk.

As a company owner, you're going to deal with many situations that are gray, legally speaking. Not every decision is mapped out; many of them will be left up to you to decide as you grow.

Attorney Spencer Reese says, "People come to the lawyer with a very specific plan or campaign or claim and ask, 'Can I do this or can I do that?' We have to look at the parameters of the law, which are often not clear, and there will always be risks associated with going in one direction or another. So you have to figure out your degree of risk tolerance. It's largely true that the greater the risk, the greater the reward, but it's also true that the greater the risk, the greater the downfall, or opportunity for downfall, as well."

Unfortunately, some people's tolerance of risk borders on the hallucinogenic. Zeek Rewards sold "penny auction" bids through what turned out to be an illegal commissioning structure to thousands of affiliates. After super-fast growth, it experienced a preternatural climb to $162 million *a month*, and subsequently crashed in August of 2012 when the North Carolina AG, the SEC and US Secret Service raided their offices, in what turned out to be one of the largest ponzi schemes in history. Thousands and thousands of people lost money and the company is in receivership.

Attorney Kevin Thompson said later in a blog post that Zeek "exploited the gray. They took a bath in it; they skinned it and made a coat out of it." The owners of Zeek had a dangerous level of risk tolerance and it ultimately led to jail time. A lot of it.

This is of course an extreme example, but the point is if you build your business on a legally shaky foundation, the potential risk is not only to you but to thousands of folks in your field. Make sure the ship is tight from the beginning.

LAUNCH LESSON #14

Be Careful with Bonuses.

There are many ways to create incentives for the field and reward them for behavior that increases volume and revenue. Careful attention should be paid to the rules around them in the states and countries where you operate.

For instance, "Three and free" programs have been popular in recent years. Lots of companies have them. The basic model is that if you're a customer for a company (not a distributor), and you refer three customers who buy, the company will give you the product for free or some other compensation in the form of product or a discount. "This violates the anti-referral laws in a whole bunch of states," says Spencer Reese. "We haven't seen any enforcement of these laws for a number of years, but that doesn't mean it isn't going to backfire at some point. Is that something you want to make the mainstay of your program? While can be effective, it rests on a shaky legal foundation. The shoe could drop at any moment, and you could lose a big chunk of your business if you rely heavily on that program.

"Fast-start bonuses" are another gray area. "About 90% of the plans I see have some sort of fast-start bonus associated with them," says Spencer. "If a distributor buys a certain product package or brings in a certain amount of volume after a certain amount of time in the business, that triggers a bonus to an upline either one or two levels up, and it's a fairly lucrative bonus. These programs look a lot like a headhunting or recruiting fee. Often they're based on the purchase of a specific pack that involves a lot of merchandise—more than the new distributor is likely to use during their first month in the program by the time their auto-ship kicks in. That's a risky situation—usually the riskiest part of a compensation plan.

"So this speaks to the design of your compensation plan. A lot of companies think, 'I have to be competitive with everyone else, and everybody else has these fast-start bonuses.' It's true—they're everywhere.

"But while not illegal, they lie in a gray area. It's a question of balancing the risk and the reward, and where you fit in the competitive marketplace. There are ways to buffer that or mitigate the risks of fast-start bonuses, but it starts with planning and structure."

Tip: As always, obtain good industry counsel to assess the risk associated with your compensation structure or product group. Make sure you obtain counsel that understands this industry. One of the riskiest decisions many new entrants make is using non-industry legal resources.

LAUNCH LESSON #15

Create a System and Provide the Tools to Support It.

When someone who wants to make a little money (or a lot of money) joins a direct selling company, the expectation is that the company will provide the systems and tools that the distributor will use to succeed in the business.

A successful sales system (not to be confused with a software system) is a series of steps or actions or processes and has two characteristics: it can be easily duplicated and provides predictable results. Developing a great sales system is a crucial part of pre-launch.

What does the selling system look like? What are its functions? How do they all come together to ensure that the volume rises, that people can make money?

The system needs to support the three R's: recruiting, retention, and revenues. It needs to be shareable and replicable. The system should be something that the field can easily interpret and follow and not need to think much about. If they just follow that system, they'll be successful.

This is the code everyone's trying to crack—building the ultimate system that will lead to assured success.

There are systems and there are tools. Videos and websites can serve as tools to build a recruiting system or a team-building system. During pre-launch, a lot of thought and training should go into developing a solid system and the tools to make it operate effectively.

Dan Jensen: "This is something that many pre-launch companies fail to see. They may have an amazing product, a wonderful USP, a great comp plan, and think they have the world by its tail. But they're not quite there yet. They have to build their systems, because that's what people will use to succeed. Companies that launch without systems in most cases fail."

It is important that 'the system' and the compensation structure agree with one another. Whatever the immediate steps to a successful start for a new recruit are, ensure that they are properly incentivized and directed toward future growth. Kevin Larson of New Earth says "It is surprising how many people will build in a manner that is completely backwards to how they get paid. This leads to frustration and regrets in a business model that has no room for either."

Dan Jensen notes the business safeguards that come with a solid system: "In any form of business there's a pretty high failure rate. There are common denominators among companies that don't make it. The franchise business is designed to reduce that rate by getting people to follow best practices for whatever business they're trying to launch. There's a pretty low mortality rate for McDonald's. The franchise works because the systems work.

"A Tupperware party plan is a system. When people join, everyone follows the same clear set of guidelines: you start by getting a list of your friends, you ask your friends if they would be willing to do a party, you do the party. At the party, the first thing you say is this, the second thing you say is that, and so forth and so on. By learning the selling system, you create predictable results."

This is what people want when they join direct selling—confidence that the systems will make them successful. The first proof is in watching the sponsors use those systems and achieve success. The second proof is in doing it themselves.

"In my opinion, that's what built Pampered Chef. They perfected their party system. It's what built them into the company that Warren Buffet bought. It wasn't because they had unique pots and pans that nobody else had. It wasn't because their comp plan was amazing. It was their selling system, and the alignment of everything they did to strengthen that selling system. To this day it carries their success."

LAUNCH LESSON #16

Target the Right People.

Another key component of pre-launch is honing your marketing message so that it attracts the kinds of people who want to be in at the very beginning of something. You're targeting a certain type of person and mindset during pre-launch.

As Rob Hawthorne says the people you want to reach in a Pre-launch may differ from those you go after post-launch. "Most people will never join a pre-launch. They follow the herd and look for proven companies that have been around for a while. They won't join a company until it's established. In the case of a pre-launch, you're not trying to enroll the masses, but rather the innovators, the forward-thinking people who are instantly able to identify with the company's vision and opportunity.

"After you launch, the targeting may change. You need to make sure that you're marketing correctly to the right person, whether it's a 35-year-old mom with two kids or a retired person looking to make some extra income. You're always crafting the vision of the company to fit people's desire for products that will help them, and the income or lifestyle potential you're going to provide."

LAUNCH LESSON #17

Embrace Modern (Online) Selling Tools.

Selling tools have changed vastly in the industry. Having your field pay for a magazine or DVD set is no longer a valid approach. That model is morphing into mobile apps, technology, and other approaches.

Richard Brooke, the founder of Oxyfresh and LifeShotz, spoke about this new world and how we have to prepare to meet it.

"Right now the industry is dominated by 50 and 60-year-olds like me. In the next five to 10 years, we'll see the industry dominated by people who are now in their 30s. They see things in a totally different way. Direct selling is going to change dramatically.

"When the old guard ages out of the system, the companies will be run by people who were raised in a totally different paradigm and communicate in a totally different way. Right now we have a demographic in direct sales who barely use email and aren't on Facebook or Instagram. For the old guard, email was a big adaptation to make. I've made one major communication shift in my entire career, and that was from handwriting every communication on a yellow tablet to using email. That was a huge transition for me, but I'm not likely to make another big communication breakthrough in my career.

Richard continues: "But by the time the younger guard is running the industry, they will have smoothly transitioned through a number of different communication modalities. Right now, we probably have five or six different methods of communicating with our distributor force. Twenty years ago, a marketing person in direct selling only needed to know about print. Today, print is worthless. Even DVDs are worthless. Tablets and most new laptops don't even have a DVD slot. Ask anyone under 30 the last time they watched a DVD or read a print magazine back to back, they won't remember. Ask a 20-year-old and you may hear 'never.'"

In addition, the revenue streams many companies have enjoyed from non-commissionable paid-for sales tools like magazines are also diminishing greatly. In what may be a sign of increasing integrity in our business, some companies are refusing to charge the field for anything but the cost of their product. Sign up fees and 30-packs of field-purchased sales tools are becoming much more the exception than the norm.

What we find now is that people would rather use online tools and/or create their own. This carries its own risk, which we'll get into later. But the idea that we're going to print material, sell it to the field, make money on it, and then have the field build their businesses with it, is dying.

The industry is embracing new tools, but it has far to go to compete in the world of Amazon and mobile shopping. And most importantly, these online media and activities are taking away from what used to be selling time for us. We need to be on the cutting edge as much as we can and use technology to entertain, inspire, and build community.

The good news? The technology for that is already here.

Most industry executives are very aware of the seismic shift toward online marketing and digital techniques used by the field and finally (thankfully) by companies themselves. In *Social Selling*, I described a future when social media becomes the center of direct selling activity, and other more traditional types of direct selling marketing take a backseat or even become obsolete.

That future is already here, only two years after I penned the book. Companies have found they are now *required* to show up well online, on Facebook and Twitter, and especially when their names are Googled. Social media and brand marketing sophistication are now the price of admission for direct sellers.

For newly launched companies and products, social media presents an opportunity to compete at the highest level alongside long-established companies. Now a new company can show just as much personality, savvy, and excitement as the big guys. Size (or history) no longer matters in marketing; it's all about the skills.

YouTube is now the second largest search engine in the world (number one if you count that it's owned by Google). People go to YouTube to seek any type of information. Your company should be there with a dedicated channel that contains great video selection. Fortunately, direct sellers have adapted quickly to online video; video marketing is a large part of our past and the jump made sense.

A less logical commitment for many companies are sites like Twitter and Instagram, which demand a new way of communicating to which many in the industry are not accustomed.

Social media is not the future; it's the present. Yet direct sellers are by and large not using it to their full advantage. They put up a Facebook page and maybe Pinterest, post here and there when the staff has time, and treat it as an afterthought. It seems to "work" and people aren't complaining. However, if you're a prospective consultant seeking a new company to join, what does a mediocre attempt at social say to them? If your social media is filled with a bunch of lame posts, boring content, or self-serving junk, they may assume that reflects the company as a whole. It's a first impression, and we all know what that means.

> Social media should be beautiful and engaging and robust and alive. You can be on Facebook, Pinterest, and Twitter, but if nothing's going on, it won't help you and may even hurt you.

Social media should be beautiful and engaging and robust and alive. You can be on Facebook, Pinterest, and Twitter, but if nothing's going on, it won't help you and may even hurt you.

The smart companies know that the more they look "on fire," the more on fire they become, and the more people will get excited about the message and want to join during the crucial launch phases. It's important that when people research you and find you online, you're really alive. That excitement, that robustness, is a crucial concept to put front and center

In sum, new companies need to put in some thinking on the front end about who their audience is and how to reach them. If you want to attract younger audiences, you're going to concentrate more on mobile and online.

That's the great thing about social selling—it's infinitely targetable. For example, social media can tell you not only the demographics of the people you're targeting, but the psychographics, interests, hobbies and so on. You can compare what they like and target what people like, rather than just who they are. That is a whole new level of targeting.

For example, as we put a recent Facebook advertising strategy for several of our clients recently, we found that a client's field reps seemed to have a fondness for the country singer Miranda Lambert. So we tested their posts and ads against others who liked her. In this case we were equally interested in demographics as we were about shared interests. And it worked out great.

Another technique we use is a Facebook function that allows you to target "lookalike" audiences to reach people who are similar to your current customers. Very cool.

Because Facebook in particular now requires advertising in order for content to be widely distributed, we regularly use these and other paid strategies, as well as "boosting" techniques, to increase our clients' followings and keep things growing. Yes, it costs more money, par for the course now on Facebook and necessary to be heard above all the noise.

> Because Facebook in particular now requires advertising in order to be successful, we regularly use these and other paid strategies, as well as "boosting" techniques, to increase our clients' followings and keep things growing.

Every single day, there's a new online tool that can benefit our industry. I read recently that 15 new social networks are created every week. That means lots of new tools that direct sellers might be able to utilize (and a lot of useless sites, too).

Additionally, the tools that we've come to rely on are changing dramatically. Facebook's utility to the industry has changed drastically just in the last year. Since becoming a public company, it is no longer a free source of social marketing for brands; it's now a pay-to-play environment. If you're going to be active on Facebook and want to maintain a market there, you will now need to pay Facebook for the privilege. This occurred essentially overnight (though there were plenty of warning signs) and upended a lot of company marketing programs.

Importantly, the requirement to continue to create good content has not gone away. Even paying to support your posts, you'll still need to continue to develop consistently good content on Facebook since you're still competing for people's attention.

So it's not just a question of new tools emerging. You'll also have to take into account the changes taking place in the tools that you're *already* used to.

We'll dice deeper into social media in later lessons as the rocket lifts further.

LAUNCH LESSON #18

Stay Flexible, and Focus on the Field.

A startup doesn't need to put in all the bells and whistles into the offering at the beginning. It's not necessary. It doesn't make sense to put too much time, money, and energy into it when you're going to change and adjust it down the road.

Ruby Ribbon CEO Anna Zornosa advises other new entrants to focus on the most important things and stay flexible so they can adapt to inevitable change.

"If you over-architect at the beginning based on what you think is going to happen, you'll lose the ability to iterate once you actually start seeing who your customer is and what she buys. So it's always a dance in launching with less than you really want, mostly because it's too expensive to build a complete vision before actually launching. If you build that complete vision too soon, you're making choices in advance of having data and experience.

"One thing that really helped us at launch was that we were extremely transparent with our stylists. For example, we were clear with them that the way we were handling returns needed to improve. We couldn't perfect the return process until we had more experience with returns, because we were so focused on making sure that our stylists were paid every month. We were very transparent about the choices we were making and promised to perfect the processes over time. As a result, we were able to build a lot of trust."

LAUNCH LESSON #19

Don't Overestimate the Value of the Back Office.

Many new companies go all out in the beginning, implementing a giant software system or deciding they're going to put every feature in the back office. They have the mistaken assumption that people spend a lot of time in the back office, moving around and doing a lot of things, but they really don't. They spend much more time in social media and email, trying to market their businesses. They might be visiting the back office every now and then to check their commission or maybe watch a training video. But the log-in rate for the back office is relatively low for most companies. Instead, a new company's money should be spent on perfecting the offering and sales tools, to get the field started off right.

LAUNCH LESSON #20

Test, Test, Test.

One of the guiding principles at Momentum Factor is testing. We test in the real world as much as possible and get as close to certainty as we can, even when the conventional wisdom says otherwise.

For instance, in our reputation defense work we're always trying to figure out what makes things rank highly on Google. We could do what 99% of search engine-related firms do, ask Google directly. Google's hope is that we follow their guidance and that little changes in their search results. But because we test everything, we validate what Google tells us and decide whether or not we think it's a good idea. The point is, for us to do our work, we need to make sure that everything we do is validated and tested.

Direct sellers should do the same. Test the product, the software, the back office, commission check runs, and everything in between. If you have a party plan, you want to hold multiple test parties to understand what the dynamics are. Don't trust your instincts or most anyone else's for that matter. You have to know if the parties are going to work. As the owner in a startup, you have to go out and find people and conduct a real party yourself to truly understand how people react to the product and what their objections are. You need to experience this firsthand. The owner has to live the experience of the consultant.

Dan Jensen echoes this advice. "I recommend twenty to thirty test parties. Not a focus group, where people are paid to tell you what you want to hear, but a real party with real people. Have your friend's wife serve as a hostess and see how people react to the products. Test the pricing, how you promote the products, and how much people pay for them.

Don't trust your instincts or most anyone else's for that matter.

"For network marketing companies, you'll need to hit the streets and gauge interest in what you're doing. If you're not party plan, you go out and try to sell your product to 20 or 30 clients. Take note of what worked and didn't work. Perfect your selling approach. Perfect your recruiting approach. Again, this is a business of systems. Systems can be duplicated and provide predictable results. It's the systems that you have to test."

Jan Gilmore encounters a lot of naïveté among startup party plan entrepreneurs with little direct selling experience.

"I ask clients: how do you know people are going to buy your product? They say, 'Oh, I've been selling this at retail, and I figure this is another way I'll be able to sell it.'

"But that doesn't mean people are going to buy the same product at a party. They may have tried focus groups, where people say they like the product and it's fairly priced. But did they put their money where their mouths are? That's the difference between a focus group and real party.

"Until you've had between 20 to 30 parties, you won't have a clue as to what will really work. What sells in your store may not sell at a party, because party success depends on many variables, like the presentation and likeability of the consultant. You need to find out what the average party brings in, what the average guest spends, and whether you can get bookings. Bookings keep people going—if I do a party and two people say they want to host one, then I'm still in business. But if I do the party and don't get a booking, then I have to start all over again and find someone to host. You need to prove you can do bookings or otherwise you'll find that people join you, do a little work, and then leave. Your business becomes a revolving door.

"People get carried away and spend money on software and compensation plans, and they haven't got a clue about whether the product sells or whether they can get bookings. If you don't know those things, you don't know how to structure a compensation plan. If you think you're going to have a $700 party but the average is $350, you may need to structure your compensation plan differently.

"The biggest mistake people make is that they don't do the testing themselves. But it's the founders who really need to be out there doing the test parties. Then you can spend money on software and everything else. But too many startups do it the other way around."

LAUNCH LESSON #21

Make Sure the Software Works.

One of the most common problems in pre-launch is on the software side. A lot of companies are preparing to launch or being pushed to launch by investors when everything isn't ready to go live.

You can't just do what Microsoft does and release a product and work the bugs out later. Let me use the gardening analogy again: any negative thing, an insect or mold, can kill the flower. A launch requires absolutely flawless implementation. A system fault that causes one missed paycheck or promised delivery date is all it takes for an otherwise eager new rep to conclude you just don't have your stuff together. And if you do make mistakes, which are inevitable, you must be transparent, react quickly, and make sure you fix it.

Software is one place where things can often go wrong. It needs to be validated and tested.

LAUNCH LESSON #22

Avoid Announcing Absolutes.

Providing deadlines and release dates is a natural thing to do in any mainstream business, but in direct selling it can cause you problems. Announcing absolute dates for launches and product releases is risky, because things happen and there are always delays. If you set your launch date for June 1, but you find a bug in your software on May 30, you've completely screwed yourself. Setting an absolute launch dates is a dangerous thing for a startup.

The commercial world does it all the time, but in our industry you can't. People are waiting and waiting for June 1. They tell all their friends about how great it's going to be, and then it doesn't happen. It wrecks the credibility of your field and company. How many times can you dash people's expectations and expect them to stick around? Very few, especially as a startup.

After a mistake, and your taking ownership of it, the field may still love you. But they're going to be more hesitant, and we don't want the field to be cautious or lacking confidence about launch. And we undermine their confidence by making promises we don't deliver, and not anticipating and planning for delays.

Once you know you have everything *absolutely* set, then maybe you put a date on it. Once you know the software's flawless, once you know your systems work and your marketing is in place, once you know the date of the event and everything's been tested multiple times, then you set an date. But not until then.

Rob Hawthorne: "On the software side, you need the pre-launch component built into your back office, so there's seamless integration once you go into your upgrade period prior to the official launch. One pre-launch I've been through was a nightmare because they had to hire dozens of people to enter every single person who converted by hand.

"Because everyone is so busy during pre-launch, people get stretched too thin and inevitably launches get delayed. There are companies that delay launch for thirty days and then another sixty days. You never hear of those companies again."

You never want to delay a launch. It's the number one momentum killer for a new company. You destroy all the trust you worked so hard to establish. You've promised people something that they so much want to believe in. When it doesn't happen, they turn their backs and move on to something else.

LAUNCH LESSON #23

Build Suspense and Excitement Out of the Gate.

There's a science around building anticipation. Steve Jobs was the master.

Jobs built suspense. He would leak out information at just the right time about an upcoming product. He would use the press to announce certain things at certain times, and stage giant events that were all over the news. He would unveil the product. Then he would add another product to make it more exciting. And at the end of his speech, he'd always say: *And one more thing*. This was his trademark. He'd have yet another great announcement at that point.

One of the things our industry does very well is build suspense and anticipation. It's critical to us because it drives excitement which leads to growth.

The buildup of suspense toward "something special" applies to both party plans and network marketing models. Handbag seller Thirty-One famously put thousands of eager enrollees on a waiting list following their initial launch, while they announced they were getting their systems more in line to handle demand. The list grew into tens of thousands as anticipation intensified, and more and more people flocked to learn what the fuss was about. When they opened up shop again a month or so later, they were already in momentum.

Whether the company was being extra careful to meet demand or, as others believe, was merely using clever marketing, the decision was a good one. This "waitlist" technique reportedly originated at Longaberger who used the technique to build suspense when they opened. Southern Living at Home did as well, and actually had people pay a small amount of money to hold their place as they planned out their company, which not only provide a small revenue stream but also mentally committed people to the cause. It was wildly successful and built great early numbers.

Suspense leads to momentum. It's a necessary part of this business. And you can do it without even having a product ready or a company to join.

LAUNCH LESSON #24

Figure Out Your Product Strategy.

The product strategy you choose is also very important. On the party plan side you'll need enough products to keep a party interesting. On the networking side, it's better to build upon a central product or two and release new products over time to continue the momentum. New products excite people and re-invigorate the field. There's a right mix, given your comp plan and business model.

A twenty year old company needs a wide variety of successive products. Companies will often run out of offshoots. If your product is a one trick pony, it's likely you won't be able to keep people interested forever. Excitement diminishes over time.

So product strategy is a huge part of momentum. Keep in mind, though, what I'm describing is a direct selling product strategy, not a commercial product strategy. They are not the same thing at all. A direct selling product strategy is different from the strategy and product roadmap taught in business school. It's specific for this industry, and it's about keeping momentum going, not building a product family where everything is related. It's always about momentum.

If your product is a one trick pony, it's likely you won't be able to keep people interested forever. Excitement diminishes over time.

What product can you release to sustain momentum over time? Most companies are reactive about this rather than proactive. They see product sales diminishing and rush to come up with something else quick. Then they end up introducing a product that's not so great or that's unrelated to what they do or doesn't hold the interest of the field. It's not a strategic, proactive move. And that costs them credibility—and momentum.

LAUNCH LESSON #25

Make the Most of Conversion Time at Pre-Launch.

During the launch phase, you typically provide a five to seven day upgrade period. That's when you want to convert as many people as possible who enrolled for free into paying distributors. About a week before the launch date, it's important to educate people about the launch packages, the benefits and costs for each, to get people and their teams ready to select the right packages. Once that window opens, there's a mad rush to convert as many people as possible during those seven days.

Rob Hawthorne: "There are advanced strategies companies can use to dramatically increase their conversion rates from free folks to paid folks during that seven day period. That's the gold dust period for a company, when hopefully there is a lot of revenue is coming in. After the conversion phase is over, pre-launch is completed and the company is ready to move forward with their business plan. That seven day period is everything they've been building up to, from the moment they had the idea for the new company or product. That is the official launch time.

"How do I add more people? What are creative and innovative ways to do that, especially online? How can the online world get people excited and engaged? There are crucial questions to ask and answer, because launch is when many companies start to lose momentum or never really gain it. Their numbers were too optimistic, they're not adding people, and they start burning cash.

"It's about creating momentum. Ideally, pre-enrollment will run for about a 30-day period. It's going to take about 30 days to get to the beginning stages of momentum. And that's when you want to time the launch, right in the beginning of momentum. The whole purpose of a pre-launch is to build up a large base of rabid fans ready to join the company and buy the products, so the company has a significant spike in revenue on day one. When you open the doors, you want a great start with thousands or tens of thousands of distributors signed up. If you're lucky and things are really hitting out there, you launch right on the crest momentum, and that's a great place to be."

LAUNCH LESSON #26

Ready for Liftoff.

You've created peaks and valleys throughout pre-launch to keep people interested, engaged, and excited about the next big announcement or event. You've had exciting announcements about products coming out, to get as many people as possible to conference calls and webinars. You've built on that excitement by letting people know about the company and compensation plan. It's all about building excitement right out of the gate, so people can share their websites and start the pre-enrollment process.

Thanks to your careful planning for months during pre-launch, you have everything in place. Now the countdown begins and you're about to lift off. Here are core best practices to keep in mind.

First and foremost, the launch must be flawless. If it isn't, you're setting in motion a series of events that will likely cause you to explode on the launchpad.

Rob Hawthorne: "Case in point. In one launch, a company's site was down 90% of the time for four days. They had brilliant programmers flying in from all over the country, trying to figure out what was going on. There was a small glitch that was causing a cascade of problems that no one could figure out. That inevitably cost them thousands, potentially tens of thousands of people during their pre-launch.

"You have to make sure you're 100% bulletproof before you pull the trigger. I recommended they delay launch for a couple of weeks and that's what they did. That bought more time. They pushed the date forward to make up for those four lost days, and no one ever knew any different."

Direct sellers tend to underappreciate time and project management skills. The overrated skills are often sales or marketing. But the ability to get things done and get them done on time is crucial to success.

Rob Snyder of Stream Energy: "You can have the field out there promoting the product and the opportunity. But if you can't fulfill on the product side of things, you're dead in the water. If people's first experience with the firm is not getting their product for a month, that's a killer.

"And this ties into the problem that too many networking companies are not founded by business people. They think that a networking firm with a direct selling premise is a guy getting up in a room and making a rousing speech. That's problematic. If you don't have everything ready to supply the products and fulfill the opportunity, you're toast."

LAUNCH LESSON #27

Don't Embarrass the Field.

One thing that often gets lost on management is the nature of our field's commitment to others. When someone joins a new company, one of the first things we teach them is to reach out to friends and family. They are putting themselves out there, sometimes exposing themselves to doubt or even ridicule. A missed shipment or a company's bad result on Google can embarrass them. They'll not only "click off" your company, but tell everyone about the experience.

If we launch something and it doesn't work, we're sapping motivation from people and sowing seeds of doubt. If your distrib utors have told family and friends how awesome the company is, but the software doesn't allow them to place an order, you've just wrecked your credibility and customer base. And, unfortunately, it's common for direct selling companies to crash that way. It happens all the time.

If you're not flawless in your execution, people will not only stop working for you but will spread the bad news. They'll call the CEO at 5 a.m. on Saturday to vent about how the company sucks. If you miss a check run, you might as well pull the plug.

If people have gone out and done what you told them to do and you don't reward them, they'll be saying, "Why am I doing this?"

Anything that pokes a hole in the balloon of motivation is bad news. And almost anything can do it. You can and will make some mistakes. Mistakes you must own and make good. But you can't make the big mistakes (or "the wrong mistakes," as Yogi Berra once said).

If you lose the confidence of your field, you're done. Turn out the lights. Game over.

LAUNCH LESSON #28

Under-Promise, Over-Deliver.

There's a tendency in the industry to be very confident and optimistic about things, even when all of the facts and data are not in yet. The data is not available on launching day, and you can't make promises without data. You won't have the data right away that you need to make decisions and policy. You can't promise what you're not certain about delivering.

Ivy Hall of Initials, Inc. reveals that exceeding expectations is key to creating momentum.

"What is momentum? It's moving a group of people to share your business with other people. That's the key to sustainable momentum. When you exceed expectations, what you do as a company becomes shareable. If you exceed expectations in providing a product or an opportunity that can impact someone's life, that's the seed for momentum."

Some companies are quick to over-promise and get people excited, without worrying about execution. That's bad business. Good business requires respectful constraint by those who are in charge.

LAUNCH LESSON #29

Don't Put Your Field in Lab Coats.

If companies are proud of their products, they'll spend a lot of time talking about them. That's especially true when companies have science in their products—that special ingredient that is proprietary, backed by clinical studies, and whose story can only be told through direct selling.

This science is part of storytelling, but if the product is a consumable or a health product, there's the danger is putting your field "in lab coats." This is when you begin to teach your field the science and hope they translate it correctly as they share the opportunity with others, placing them in an awkward and non-believable position. Not only will they be less effective, but it also puts the company at risk for health claims, the kryptonite of the nutritional company.

You don't want to put your distributor in the position of figuring out what the science is and then communicating that to people. They will likely get it wrong and be non-compliant when they do it.

Dan Jensen supports this notion:

"If the founder of the company has a Ph.D. in naturopathic medicine, and he's out there explaining how the product works, and it takes him 45 minutes to go through all the clinical evidence, he may have strengthened people's faith in the product, but he hasn't strengthened the story. A non-scientist has to be able to explain the product. It has to be really simple—simple enough for people to get it and simple enough for people to duplicate it."

At the same time, science has a crucial role to play. Products usually need something unique or proprietary to really make it. Otherwise, if it's really successful, other companies will knock it off and your product could end up in Walmart at half the price. We saw this in the 1990s with Monavie and the acai berry, along with many other natural supplements since. It's the truth that in direct selling we very often introduce the public to a fantastic product, which, once it takes off, is duplicated in mainstream commerce. We are innovators; to survive we need to *always* be innovating. And proprietary products backed by science can fuel that innovation.

LAUNCH LESSON #30

Embrace Social Media During Launch.

People want to know: how do I grow my new company?

Industry veterans can tell you that our business has shifted and is now coalescing around social media. Why? It's where the people are. It's where they're working, sharing, telling others about their opportunities, and spending a *lot* of their time. It has to be on fire from the start.

Today, the social presence of a company ends up being its nucleus, and that's something many in industry still don't realize. Many companies think of social media as an afterthought, but it's critical to us, and represents an opportunity for a company to scale its mindshare with the field and customers. Out of the gate, your social media should be on par with any existing direct selling company or better.

At this writing, 1.4 billion people use Facebook, 700 million use Twitter, 200 million use Instagram, and 70 million use Pinterest. How can companies tap into these huge markets during launch to tell people about their businesses and get them to join? How can they use social media to communicate with distributors? How can they use social selling to fuel momentum during launch and beyond?

These are big and important questions.

During launch, people will wait to see whether a company has its game together. Some might be leaders in another company thinking about joining your company because they love its products. If the new company looks like it doesn't know what it's doing on social media, they may just sit on the sidelines.

And that's a problem. Because if they wait, your company loses these leaders. You lose your momentum and it's that much harder to get off the ground.

LAUNCH LESSON #31

Social Selling Is Not a Fad, It's a Revolution.

In *Social Selling* I wrote of the revolution in social media upon us in this industry. One of the driving themes of that book was that social media, being structurally very similar to direct selling, is made for our business. Other industries were decimated by the advent of social media, but because of our unique model and emphasis on the importance of relationships, we were made for this new era. And the opportunity exists to grow far beyond the limits we perceive today.

Since writing my previous book, the industry has come a long way to embrace social, but we're not quite there. We've gone from ignoring it, to acknowledging it, to treating it as another marketing tool. The next step is to see social media as a central function of our companies, distinct from marketing.

I have one client who cannot seem to make that distinction. They tend to want to apply traditional print marketing techniques to their social. Their program is overseen by a more traditional marketing director who has limited knowledge of social, so naturally their images and videos reflect a "positioning" mindset and their communications reflect it.

If you accept that social media is central to your company's future growth (and you should), it deserves its own budget and dedicated resources. The ideal way to treat social at corporate would be as a separate function, a peer to marketing, finance, or operations, appropriately staffed with communicators, creators, and inspirational types, not just marketers.

A new client of ours is an old-line direct seller, been in the business for 25 years. What keeps them up at night is not being relevant anymore. The older generation of executives is worried about keeping up with the younger set. And they should be worried.

Even most companies in our industry who get it, *still don't really seem to get it.* Most direct sellers can set up a nice Facebook page. They can tweet exciting news about their products and can run contests. They're doing what everyone else is doing.

Case Study: ViSalus: Leveraging New Technology On Old Ideas

ViSalus, which markets products in the weight loss and fitness category, is a great example of a company whose marketing struck a chord, with incredible success. After several years of hard times and missteps, they eventually hit it big, really big. Just as social media was beginning to reach the masses, they embraced and leveraged it in brilliant fashion.

By combining social media as a core part of their system, free samples, and a compelling "three and free," their momentum exploded. Although they've recently receded significantly, they experienced astronomical growth numbers for some time.

No one will replicate what they did, although many have tried. They were fortunate in their timing, and boosted their growth by fully embracing social media and using it to expand the reach of their message.

One of the things that they did really well was drilling the 'three and free' concept in a big way, so much so, that it seemed like a new concept. They attracted many people who had never been involved in direct selling before. They attracted the masses, which is rare in this industry.

When they first launched, they had one product, which was their weight loss shake. And they used social proof in a smart way. People took before and after pictures of dramatic weight loss and posted them on Facebook. The message was, "If I can do this, you can too." The photos went viral, generating a lot of curiosity and excitement about the product. That was their system for getting people to join.

It was a hard-hitting marketing message that people could easily understand. Take your picture now and again in 90 days. They developed contests and their 'challenge' around this concept. "Who had the biggest transformation in 90 days? Post it!"

Once they were off and running with momentum, they sustained it by famously staging a string of events led by the founders in 70 different cities in a very short time. A massive logistical and production effort for their event team, and they were packing houses.

Eventually, like all manned rockets, ViSalus came down to Earth. With increased competition, the loss of some major leaders, and product controversies, they have scrambled recently to recapture some of their former magic. But no one argues that they created a momentum powerhouse within a short time by combining the most effective direct selling techniques, both old school and new.

***

Now that we've covered the best practices of launch, let's turn to the next crucial stage of momentum—accelerating through the atmosphere's friction and escaping gravity. It's a phase that has its own unique set of challenges, dangers, and opportunities. Some companies have spectacular liftoffs but never reach orbit, while others soar through the sky and reach the heavens quickly.

Let's find out why.

PART TWO

Acceleration and Escaping Gravity.

Acceleration is a critical time for a direct selling company. As in rocketry, breaking through to the next stage is often the trickiest and riskiest part of the journey. Companies need signifcant power to remain skyward, to break the grip of gravity and escape the atmosphere.

All systems must be go and there can't be any major failures. Just as we need to be flawless during launch, we need to be flawless during acceleration as well. Otherwise, gravity will teach us a hard lesson.

Too often, as a company finds itself accelerating and getting into momentum, the engines malfunction. It could be operational, from being unable to handle the growth, or financial, from being unable to fund the inventory and operation as it grows. Or it could be technical, as the software starts to creak and groan. If the mad growth we want is actually happening, the systems in place need to be able to handle that growth.

In my opinion, the growth curve is more a squiggly line. You're going up, and inevitably you're coming back down at least for a while. At that point you're going to hit something that will make the growth curve go up again, like a new product or an event, and then it might come back down once more. You'll rarely see a constantly ascending "hockey stick line" of growth in a direct selling company. If you do see growth like that, you're probably going to have a hockey stick going down in the other direction when the company isn't able to keep up with the growth or other conditions change. Perhaps another company has copied whatever drove that growth, and now it's driving them and not you.

So over the long-term life cycle of a company, growth is going to diminish. If you come up with one product that's really hot, go with it until growth begins to decline. Then, according to your product strategy, you come out with a new product that may happen to coincide with a national event. By reinventing innovation, you keep momentum going.

How long it will take the rocket to reach orbit is hard to know. Kody Bateman, CEO of SendOutCards, tells me that it "typically takes a company a couple of years to really get their feet wet, to get things running right in order for them to get into the acceleration phase."

In this section, we'll look at best practices in acceleration: what direct sellers need to do to grow their businesses, and what risks, temptations and fallout (legal in many cases) they need to avoid. How can companies grow in healthy ways over the long term, rather than of boosting their performance through dubious techniques?

As Ivy Hall of Initials, Inc. puts it, "The core of momentum is really about creating energy and action behind what you're offering. A lot of people think of momentum as something external to the company. But it's really reflective of internal processes, internal products, and the opportunity you're offering."

Let's take a look at some of those key internal processes.

ACCELERATION LESSON #1

Accelerate Organically, Not Artificially.

Growth has to be organic, not artificial. Too many direct sellers fuel their growth artificially. But like a sugar high, it doesn't last and can even be hazardous to your health. You always want to build a company with people excited and eyes open, who are motivated to build based on your company's foundations and principles, versus a mere money play. Artificial growth has become rampant in the industry and is unhealthy for the companies who do it, and the industry at large.

Companies should strive to build a grassroots organization whose members join for the right reasons.

One of the common temptations in emerging companies is to "buy" leaders from other companies by paying bonuses to people to come over with their teams. As growth wanes or stalls, a company may begin to covet the revenue and potential multiplier the field leaders *may* bring via their influence over established teams in the field. Owners often get dollars in their eyes and instantly envision the volume that the new leaders can generate. Someone comes in claiming to have made six figures per month in revenue in their last company, and it can be hard to turn that away when there are bills to pay.

But in nearly all cases, it doesn't work out.

A leader might say to an owner, "For me to come over, I need $10,000 a month for each of four people on my team to be able to build a leg of 3,000 people." Beyond the legal or ethical implications of this approach, the problems are numerous. First, on average, fewer than a third of the people on their team will come over with them, so you have to discount by at least 70% a leader's ability to do that. Secondly, if you pay a leader's expenses to bring a big team over, then that team is not coming because of the product, the story, the founder, and the people. They're coming over because someone encouraged them to because they got paid. It's unnatural and a conflict of interest. In the end there will be three losers: the company the people are leaving, the company gaining people temporarily, and the distributors jumping ship.

In addition, there are so many negative byproducts to all this, including lawsuits (almost inevitable when a big leader leaves under non-competes) and, possibly worse, negative online chatter arising from that extends out and affects people who are not even involved. All of a sudden the wonderful business they thought they joined has become a rat's nest of accusations and negativity.

Sometimes the team movement is supported by both companies and they called it a merger, like when a company is going out of business and their sales field is negotiated over to another company (usually in a financial deal with the "merged" company's owners. This is occasionally successful at first because both companies ostensibly support it, but, generally speaking, if a company doesn't have the products and opportunity to attract enough people to grow the business organically, without needing to goose it with an artificial bump, they may want to question what they're doing in the business. The idea that you can bid for leaders to bring great volume over to sustain a business has proven to be a failing strategy. Yet companies keep doing it, over and over again.

If a company doesn't have the products and opportunity to attract enough people to grow the business organically, without needing to goose it with an artificial bump, they may want to question what they're doing in the business.

Another way of accelerating artificially is by boosting your volume internally with the field, using the comp plan or bonusing product volume. That's almost a regular *modus operandi* for many companies: "Oh, we need to do a promotion so we can get more volume to make our numbers at the end of the month." Some of these approaches are healthy while others are not. While it's great to introduce new products to the field as we've described, some serve merely to pump up excitement for a short while and end up cannibalizing the current products that are actually selling, many on monthly autoship.

Few people will just keep adding money on top of what they're already spending on product. Kevin Larson of New Earth says, "Keep in mind that there is a practical limit to the amount of money that any particular distributor will place on a autoship. "Although you may want to roll out new products to increase the size of the autoship this almost never turns out to be the case. New products should expand your audience and attract new demographics. Try to avoid making your distributors choose between the product they love vs. the product that is new."

Try to avoid making your distributors choose between the product they love vs. the product that is new.

When companies buy distributors or pick off leaders from other companies, it can be a nice shot in the arm, but long term it doesn't do any good. Those people are going to leave. If they didn't join for the right reasons they're just mercenaries, and sooner or later they're going to do the same thing to you. They'll go on to the next hot deal when they're ready.

The healthiest way to grow is to buckle down and build it right. There are few silver bullets in this business other than true, organic momentum.

ACCELERATION LESSON #2

Don't Believe Your Own Hype.

My friend Richard Brooke, founder of Oxyfresh and LifeShotz, says one challenge facing direct sellers is the temptation to create momentum through a shallow marketing message, which he calls "regurgitated hype."

"Most fast-rising companies in direct selling are growing fast because they're promoting how fast they're growing. It's systemic. It's in the culture. ViSalus was one example, and before them it was Monavie, and before them there was Noni. There's always a company that exemplifies the philosophy: *Let's challenge our sales force to grow as fast as they possibly can.* The things that become important are how fast you rank and advance, how many people you recruit, how much money you make, and how you promote all of this on Facebook and social media. You create a fever pitch and the company catches on fire and starts growing at a record-setting pace.

"And as soon as there's some tangible, measurable evidence of 'record setting' growth, the company shifts its marketing message. No longer is the focus on the products or the opportunity, or on the company's mission and values. Instead, the marketing message becomes: *Look at us, we're the fastest growing company in the industry. We just had another record-setting month. We give more cars away than any other company in the industry. Blah blah blah.*

"There are all kinds of hype, but the worst kind is when your message has no meat in it, when it's only rehashing your own hype of how fast you're growing. The problem with that strategy is that no company maintains momentum indefinitely. By definition, momentum has a cycle. And when you've lost momentum, when your growth this year is not as good as last year, you look pretty stupid if your only sales message is how fast you're growing. That's when your distributors leave because they don't know what to say to prospects. They don't know what to say to their sales force. They were raised on a shallow marketing message, and now they have nothing to say."

The same thing happens, Brooke pointed out, when the marketing message is based on product hype.

"A company claims they have the best energy drink and all these famous people endorse it. Well, what happens two years down the line when somebody else does a better job at promoting their energy drink? What do you say then?

"The biggest challenge for gaining and maintaining momentum in direct selling is crafting a marketing message that doesn't come back to bite you and doesn't sabotage you when the momentum cycle shifts. As marketers, we need our own authentic message that can't be worn out by somebody else. Nowhere in our message should we say we have the best product, the best compensation plan, the fastest growing company, or the best opportunity.

"Your marketing message is who you are authentically. No one else can copy that. The only claim you should be making is 'this is who we are, this is what we stand for, this is what we're building.' You shouldn't compare yourself to other companies or other products. There are a lot of great companies and great products. We should encourage people to find the product and company that's right for them.

"When you have that kind of message, you're not going to end up sabotaging yourself. Your sales force won't be looking at how fast you're growing or how you compare to the next guy. Those things are not going to be as important to them."

Your marketing message is who you are authentically. No one else can copy that. The only claim you should be making is 'this is who we are, this is what we stand for, this is what we're building.

ACCELERATION LESSON #3

Remove the Friction.

Another important lesson offered by people I interviewed was the need to remove friction from the buying and selling process. When it's easy for the field to sell and customers to buy, growth is more easily accelerated.

Traditionally, we have thrown quite a few hurdles in the path of the potential enrollee. Scary looking contracts and policies, sign-up labyrinths, egregious enrollment fees, and other barriers have smothered excitement.

In the past, this was overcome with support from an upline sponsor who was right there to walk them through all of this. The difference now is that many enrollees don't have a readily available sponsor to help. They joined, in many cases, on their own, without much assistance. Therefore, we need work even harder to make it easy for them.

In the last few years, one of the most effective ways to remove friction has been mobile apps. The ability to present on the go, tied with productivity apps and a mobile office is a perfect solution for our businesses. While slow to adopt, the industry has recently begun to do serious work in this area.

Why? The field has demanded it. In *Social Selling* I devoted an entire section to Millennials and the need to meet them where they are—on mobile and social media. Today there is little excuse for any company not to offer a robust mobile app to their field. The costs are relatively minor and the technology is mature enough to invest. And an investment is worthwhile.

Kimberly Cornwell, founder and CEO of Celadon Road, agrees that adapting to the field and customer is key. Sometimes joining solo is just how some people want it.

"Some women want that consultant contact," Kimberly told me, "while other women just want their product and don't want to call anyone. They're happy if they can just place an order through their phone. So we're trying to adapt to that customer preference. I'm that kind of person myself. While I like the consultant contact, when I need something and don't have the time to talk to someone, I can just place the order. And we want be able to provide that option to customers.

"This also streamlines the consultant's business because they don't have to take the time to get the order and credit card information. It's also going to help at events, where consultants have been using Square to process credit cards. When they use Square, they get charged for it. With the new mobile app there's just one processing for the consultants, as opposed to using Square and then placing the order. It's a good thing for them."

Another company that takes the friction of out of the selling process is a new apparel startup called Lula Roe. They have a unique model that buys fabric remnants and converts them into women's skirts and dresses. They have removed much of the friction by simply shipping an entire box of product that ladies can try on at a party. No worries about multiple SKUs, preferences, sizes, or colors. What actually arrives is a surprise and makes for a great party, and whatever is not sold is returned to the company. That fun is a big part of the momentum equation.

"The magic for Lula Roe," said Terrel Transtrum who works with them, "is when you receive your big box of products. Neighbors will actually come over to your house and be there to see what's in it. And the party has a lot of energy, with women trying on clothes and telling each other how good they look. At some parties they'll sell a hundred skirts or more. The company has a structure in place that allows that to happen, and the momentum is then created by the people at the party."

Lula Roe's removal of major hurdles (advance ordering, returns, catalogs, advanced inventory management, hundreds of SKUs) removes the friction and leads to more excitement. It's a win-win.

ACCELERATION LESSON #4

Focus on Retention.

Recruiting and retention are the lifeblood of direct sellers. Think about how much it costs to recruit and train a new person, compared to the people who are already trained, know what you're doing, and are already excited. If I had to choose between recruiting and retention, I would certainly start with retention.

But a lot of companies are more focused on the recruiting side because that's where their skills lie or what they've done since they started up and it worked. They may have a lot of turnover in their base because they're not working on retention as much as they could.

Jan Gilmore spoke to me about churn in the industry, and what could be done to reduce attrition and retain good people.

"This revolving door is a problem with every company today. Their websites say, 'Work your own hours. No commitment. No quotas to meet.' It sounds too easy and there are few expectations.

"There have to be expectations and consequences. Most companies don't have them, and that's a real problem.

"Executives will throw up their hands and say, 'Well, how can I manage volunteers? I don't pay them a salary. How can I tell them what to do?'

"The answer is to get people into the right habits. Whatever the business model is, whatever method you're using, it works. Most people will rise to the occasion if they know what's expected of them, or at least they will try. But if there are no expectations, why should someone bother trying?

"Expectations have to be established in your initial contact with people. Companies are all over the place recruiting people, but never think about a qualifying process that will determine the person's real interest. Do they ever intend to do any work? Or are they really a customer in disguise? What's their commitment? What's their 'why?' Why do they want to do this? Companies recruit without asking these questions, and they end up with a hundred people on their team and only 20 who are working. And it's discouraging to try to get hold of the other 80."

ACCELERATION LESSON #5

Protect Your Brand and Reputation Online.

Very often its the hidden or subtle things that can do in a business. One challenge that directly affecs the field daily that we might not feel at the home office is a negative online reputation. Negative occurences and public perception have a big impact on our bottom line, because distributors and the people they attempt to enroll are so sensitive to them.

Joining a direct seller is what we marketers call a "considered purchase." It is a big commitment. People know they will need to spend a lot of time and at least some money in getting started. They do their research.

When someone is introduced to your opportunity, what is the very first thing they do? They check Google. Next? They check their social networks. "Who are these guys? Who is involved with this company that I know? What do other people think of them?" They want to make sure it's a wise decision. They ask their spouses, who may take it upon themselves to do deeper research, sometimes even looking for reasons *not* to join the company.

With Google and Facebook, any company or product is instantly searchable. And because of that, the credibility of your company and field is on the line *all* the time. Google any direct seller and the search results will very often bring up negative or counter-productive links and videos, with titles like "XYZ Company: Is it a scam?" and "Don't join XYZ Company until you read this!" As most of us know, this is the work of people seeking to divert attention. This is very, very common in the industry, and I'll explain why in a minute.

If a rep has to fight that battle, along with the battle of selling to friends and family, joining a direct seller becomes really daunting. So the onus is on us to make sure our Google results are clean, or at least neutral and not negative, and that Facebook and our social media presence are monitored, robust and positive.

These are often tough things to accomplish. You might have a brand or founder's name that carries some baggage. Or you may have disgruntled ex-reps. People get in, they think they're going to make a ton of money and don't, and being the social-centric consumers they are, start trashing the company. Online blowback is very common from people who don't make it. And it's a hard thing to prevent or overcome online.

The universal "common area" for your brand name is in Google search. It is the first, and I would argue, most important place to focus your image enhancement efforts.

We had a recent client, a CEO who made a mistake many of us make: he hired the wrong guy. He had to fire the person, who turned out to be of the really spiteful variety. The terminated employee vowed he would do his best to destroy the CEO and his company any way he could. The first thing he did was create a lie-filled, vitriolic post about the CEO on a major complaint forum. He then hired search engine firms to boost the post so it ranked at the top for the CEO's name. It was one of the worst cases we've seen as far as attacks go, and the cost to the company was incalculable.

The universal "common area" for your brand name is in Google search. It is the first, and I would argue, *most* important place to focus your image enhancement efforts. Your website branding or packaging efforts are not nearly as important. Hard to believe, but in terms of recruiting and retention, it's true.

A direct seller can address this exposure by ensuring that its Google "mirror" remains clean—that what Google mirrors back is positive and affirms the rep's decision to join your company.

It can be done, contrary to the opinion of many consultants who may not be experienced in this area. I recently attended an industry event where the keynote speaker was presented as a social media expert. When asked by a company executive in the audience what could be done about an attack blog that comes up when the company name is searched, the speaker said, "Oh, I'm sorry, nothing can be done about that. You have to learn to live with it." The executive looked really disappointed, it was like she'd been told she had an incurable disease. I wanted to shout *It's not true!* (Well, I did tweet it.)

No matter what you've heard, Google results most certainly *can* be changed in your favor. It takes time and expertise, but as long as Google uses a computer algorithm to rank things (which is forever), search results can be influenced, often very much so.

Weighing the cost/benefit, when you look at the direct costs in recruiting, retention, brand equity, and field morale, fixing a negative result in your Google results is an absolute no-brainer. The money spent making your reputation clean far exceeds the losses you'll incur if it's negative. Shockingly, little investment is commonly made on this.

Go now, Google your company and the names of your founders and executives. What do you see in the first few pages? Likely a brandjacker video or two. Maybe a negative forum like PissedConsumer.com or Scam.com. Maybe an attack blog or two. Perhaps there are videos with "scam" in the title. Maybe a negative story, litigation, or regulatory action from the past is creeping up on the page.

So how do you clean that kind of stuff up?

I'm going to into some detail about this, because it's important.

First I'll explain how Google works, and then how a firm like ours works to make search results better. It's a pretty interesting story.

When you type in a keyword on Google, it presents you with the most relevant listings for that keyword. If I type in, "Where can I buy a chair?" Google wants to present me with places nearby or online where I can buy a chair that is relevant, as much as possible, to you and what you are searching for. Google is forever building an algorithm to make the results it presents ever more specific to you as a user.

Therefore, Google will give weight to anything that indicates that the search result was relevant to you. This complex algorithm takes into account your friends, your social media, geographic location, past searches, the type of keywords you plug in, or even the way you ask your question. It takes into account everything related to you and the question you ask, and tries as hard as it can to give you the most relevant results.

This is Google's goal, because if it provides you with relevant results, it can also give you relevant advertising around those results. Maybe you'll pick one of the ads in order to buy the product you're looking for. And that's how Google makes its money. Make sense so far?

So Google's everyday result is, "I want to show you things that are relevant." In our industry, what Google finds relevant are the following: lots of conversation around a topic, and people talking on social media, on blogs, or in forums, where there's a banter back and forth using keywords. Google is going to favor those conversations that relate to the keyword because they're going to say, "This is hot, this is something happening, this is something that's relevant for the keyword. So, as a user, you should see this result because it talks about this particular keyword in this way."

That can be both good and bad. A company's reviews are related to this search, so Google is going to pull up reviews as a relevant result and response. That can be really tough for our companies, because very often we might endure some bad reviews. If you plug in XYZ Company, which 99.9% of people will do—*I want to learn more about XYZ Company because Mary introduced me to it, and I need to learn about this company before I consider joining it*—the second result might be a link on Scam.com, where someone is running a forum centered on whether XYZ Company is a scam or not. Your eagerness to join that company just dropped by half.

If you click on that link, your excitement may fall even further as you read, "Don't join this company. I put my money up, and nothing happened. They just scammed me out of my money, and only idiots would join this." (That's a real quote I found easily with a quick search, by the way.) That's all it takes.

In seconds, you went from an eager prospective enrollee to someone who is now wary and reluctant.

So you call Mary, who introduced you to the company, and say, "Hey, Mary, sorry to say this but my husband says I really can't join right now." Mary is not going to hear about the scam claim because you don't want to embarrass her with that information. At that point you just want to be on your way. Mary has lost not only a fresh recruit, but has to work that much harder to convince people about the quality of her opportunity.

And Mary chalks up one more "no."

Can you feel the sadness? Now calculate this across all your reps and everyone they introduce to the company.

If there's any message I can deliver in this section, it's that a clean showing on Google is an extremely important factor in the success of any direct seller. It's unfathomable how much money in the industry is left on the table, and how much more never makes it there, when negative search results cause people to "click off" or not join.

It's critical to make sure your Google results and social media presence are positive and clean. Removing that objection is one of the most important things you can do to help your field. When your online presence is clean, they don't have to explain themselves or lose people because of some false claim or other nastiness.

So the goal is to make positive things relevant and negative things not relevant when Google presents results on a keyword search. It's very hard to do because Google gives a lot of weight to what people are talking about or up in arms about, and your company has zero control over what they're debating online. Google thinks, "Hey, this is a relevant result. People are talking about it, so that means that people want to know about it."

And if one of the bad links gets in the top ten, it becomes a vicious cycle. People click on it, read it, and that creates more debate. And the link stays on top because the people clicking on it have continuously validated it.

In our work at Momentum Factor we use sophisticated techniques, as well as on and offline strategies and methods, to attack various types of online negativity. Every case is different. Some require a technical approach, others a legal or public relations effort, or even just knowledgable copywriting. Our job is to ensure the first two pages are clean or neutral in what Google returns for that brand or executive's name.

ACCELERATION LESSON #6

Your Online Compliance is Mission Critical.

Multiple agencies regularly monitor direct sales activities—of this there is no doubt.

Nearly every country you will operate in will have a regulator in charge of consumer protection. Some are more aggressive than others. In India, which seems like a wild west of schemes and out of proportion enforcement, company executives often find themselves in jail with little to no warning. Other countries go after the distributors themselves.

In the US, The Food and Drug Administration regulates nutritional products, food-based products, and cosmetics. The Federal Trade Commission regulates the financial aspects of the business, ensuring that companies are not going to make it a money or recruiting game, but are ready to market products and pay a commission to those who sell them.

State Attorneys General offices are also very interested in our companies. If a company appears to be unethical or lacking integrity, or has received multiple complaints, it's possible that an AG looking to build a political career as a consumer watchdog may target it. For example, Montana has become nearly a no-go state for any network marketing company. Tough licensing and enforcements makes it almost not worth it to do business there.

Again, it's absolutely necessary for companies to make sure that reps are in line with policies and procedures and that they are enforced. The goal is to ensure things are safe and secure, not only from a brand perspective, but from a regulatory perspective.

For instance, it's illegal in the US for a distributor to post images of paychecks on Facebook with the line "I made $10,000 last month and you can too!"

You have to monitor that behavior and put a stop to it. A lot of companies don't realize the gravity of unchecked distributor claims, and some will feel a regulator's wrath. Make sure it's not you.

You have to monitor that behavior and put a stop to it. A lot of companies don't realize the gravity of unchecked distributor claims, and some will feel a regulator's wrath. Make sure it's not you.

A classic example of this was the case of Dallas-based Mannatech, a publicly-traded direct seller of nutritional products. In the mid-2000's, Mannatech endured not only a class-action securities lawsuit based on false distributor claims, but also a campaign by the Texas AG, who ultimately prevailed in a civil complaint. The company has recovered since, but not without a lot of pain along the way.

Keep in mind the company itself *never* made a false claim; the claims were allegedly made online by their distributors, who probably had little idea they were doing anything wrong. (The problems reportedly stemmed from one cancer claim on a distributor blog.) But the company was still on the hook for those claims and it cost them dearly.

Such is the nature of our business. As unfair as it may seem for a company to have to monitor everything reps say and do, especially on the vast expanse of the Internet, that's the way it is. The law does not differentiate between the company and the rep; field and home office are one and the same.

Miraculously, Mannatech survived this uncomfortable period in their history and have done well since. Many other companies would have folded with the very first letter of inquiry from a regulator. Why? Because when made public, that letter can suck the motivation out of everyone charged with selling that product. If a rep sees that the FTC is investigating his company, and he's having trouble selling anyway, what is he going to do? He's going to stop working. Add to that the eager competitors waiting in the wings to share their misfortune and seize opportunities, and suddenly revenue, retention, volume, and morale drop through the floor.

It takes only a single negative event to make a crucial portion of your field stop working and stop reaching out to people. So you can't afford even an *interest* from a regulatory agency, let alone an investigation.

If you're not consistently identifying and responding to compliance threats, from searching the vast Internet all the way up to regular compliance training for the field on what they should and shouldn't be doing, you could be sitting on a time bomb.

In our firm's compliance monitoring practice we are seeing a heightened level of interest from the regulatory agencies in the industry, and more regulations are sure to come, because that's the environment we're in. The US is swinging toward more scrutiny and rules about what we can and can't do. A company that's not doing all it can to enforce and monitor what's going on, especially online, is at risk.

The reality is that the pendulum is swinging and regulation is ratcheting up right now. We see it in some of the investigations and even company closures currently underway. We see it in China, which has investigated multiple companies for consumer fraud and punished them severely. In fact, due to heated regulation, China may no longer be the growth market for us we had hoped.

The current administration in the US is decidedly consumer focused, and I predict more intensive regulatory scrutiny and high-profile actions are in our near future. The Herbalife investigation, if it does not go their way, could force major changes in the business models of a significant portion of the industry, and will have public ramifications as well. Whether we like it or not, this is something companies have to address, and it's mission critical, at this stage right now, to make sure that our house is completely in order.

ACCELERATION LESSON #7

Launch New Products—or Fade Away.

Those in direct selling know that launches are not only about new companies.

This industry is defined by launches and re-launches, new products, new promotions, and the next big thing.

It's about doing something new *all the time*. It means always having something new to promote, to talk about, to keep people excited.

To the extent that you don't constantly reinvent and launch new things, you can wither away with a static message or offering. We know that once the excitement of a product or promotion or an event starts to decline, you must introduce something new to get people excited again—a comp plan enhancement, new selling tools, a mobile app, or perhaps a new proprietary ingredient.

Outsiders to the business wonder: why are we always in startup mode? Can't we just start a business, sit back, and watch it grow?

No. Target Stores can do that, but a direct seller can't. Target can have a drop in sales this month and pick it up again next month. If you drop off in direct selling, you may not get those sales back again because it takes a lot more work to regain momentum. That's why momentum is so important—it feeds off itself and keeps you moving forward. The same works in reverse. Something that takes momentum away can do so for quite a long time, until you figure out how to turn it around.

Other industries aren't launching all the time because they can't. How much excitement is HP going to create when they come out with a new computer? They're not going to be able to get 8,000 people crammed into a stadium jumping up and down and wearing funny clothes. Only *we* can do that!

Successful companies shift their mindset from becoming product companies to becoming launch marketing companies. They're in perpetual launch mode, constantly launching new products, people, and events. That's their business model. The companies that have done extremely well over the years have mastered that—Amway, Herbalife, Mary Kay. They've become really good not only at launching numerous products, but at launching events, sharing success stories, and building excitement.

Some company owners believe they're just a product company. And if that's what they want, direct selling is probably not the right business model for them. They may be better off marketing their products to Walgreens or Target.

ACCELERATION LESSON #8

Innovate Your Product Launch System.

Companies sometimes don't appreciate how important product launches are. Products are introduced at events because companies need something exciting around which to base the event. Some companies get into the business with one product without really thinking about expansion down the line.

We judge the future success of a company on the basis of how they can expand from one product over time. There has to be a strategy—we're going to start with this product and then expand to this line. You don't need to know what the products are, but you need to know what the opportunities are.

The industry should embrace new and innovative approaches to launching products. Rob Hawthorne describes one such strategy.

"Most companies announce new products at events. They use that as the carrot. Or maybe they launch a product every quarter or every year, and build their big events around that. That's definitely one approach and there's nothing wrong with it. It gets people to attend the event and builds their excitement, and they go back home and tell their downline organization.

"But how many people, on average, out of a network marketing company of 10,000 people, attend those conventions? I don't know if it's 10%, but let's say it's 1,000 people. Their launch window at the event is maybe a few minutes to an hour. The buildup to the product is typically a nice video with fast music that gets everyone excited, and everyone's fired up.

"Here's the problem: it fires up 10% of their company. Why not do a product launch similar to a company launch? Put together a 30-day campaign to launch the product to all 10,000 people. That way they get 10,000 people fired up, compared to 10%."

There's definitely an art to releasing products and the intervals at which you do that. Everything has a bell curve of excitement. And when you see the excitement start to tail off on the back side of the bell curve, you should be ready with your next product, your next event. You're looking reignite the field.

"Launch the product with a full-blown launch process, just like you're launching a company," says Rob. "Let's say a company sells skincare products for the face. Let's say they have a new product for the ears. They would go through a 30-day launch sequence, and anyone in the network who purchases the new product during that time gets it for say, 50% off. Or the company could offer 100,000 sample packages, first come, first served, so consultants can get 50 packages to share with their friends. The goal is to get that special offer in front of them and generate a lot of revenue.

"At the end of the day, if conducted correctly, launches are revenue-generating opportunities. Here's an opportunity for a product launch to generate a lot more revenue. And if it's a product that happens to have samples, that's a homerun, because now you're getting hundreds of thousands of samples to those 10,000 people, who can begin sharing with their friends.

Companies can do product packages that are commissionable or non-commissionable, that are priced as low as possible, to create a lot of volume and drive a lot of commissions. There are dozens of different things companies can do to create the offer. The offer needs to be critical and timely to generate a lot of revenue, either in immediate commissions or commissions down the road."

But there are also cautions to keep in mind.

Dan Jensen: "Constant buildup, yes. But it's just as critical that distributors have an environment of constancy, where the rules of compensation don't change, where the environment in which they work is predictable. If constant buildup means constantly changing things, that's not good. If you're constantly changing things, your sales force has no anchor. You might have amazing products, but you don't have the environment of constancy and predictability desperately needed in direct selling companies. That's the flip side of constant buildup."

ACCELERATION LESSON #9

Be Wary of Changing the Formula.

If you're in acceleration and trying to escape gravity, try not to do anything that's going to screw it up, because falling back to Earth is not pleasant.

It's obvious that companies should be on top of how things are going and adjust along the way. But companies need to take a really hard look at any decisions they make that will affect the field's production, product quality, shipping times, or commissions—anything at all that will change the field experience. Sticking to the formula is the challenge of acceleration.

If you're in acceleration, get out of the way and keep feeding it fuel. Keep doing what you're doing, escape the atmosphere, and get into orbit.

Mistakes are often made at this stage, as companies do everything they can do hang on to the momentum. So they tweak here, change there, or try to correct earlier decisions that results in less profit once they were growing. So they'll change a product or compensation mid-flight because they're not seeing enough money. More often than not, it's these kind of changes that cause acceleration to fail.

I'll give you an example. Last year, a new cosmetics direct seller was doing very well, about $10-$11 million a month over several months. Soon management became impatient and wanted more, so they decided to save on what they perceived was expensive manufacturing and changed the vendor who made their product. The new product, which underwent limited testing (there's that word again), was defective, and they experienced massive returns. Their field was embarrassed and immediately stopped selling. Murphy's law in action. The company fell apart from that one little mistake. It was a classic example of killing the golden goose—focusing on operational efficiency or squeezing out more profit, rather than protecting the product and field

As we discussed in the Launch section, Mistakes in our industry have a far greater impact than many other industries. If Wal-Mart puts out a faulty product, to some extent they're shielded by their corporate size. Their sales won't just stop. When Microsoft releases Windows updates, they can fix software bugs on the fly. And that works when you have a near monopoly on a market or are so big that one mistake can't hurt you.

Another example would be changes in the comp plan. If people have been making good money and suddenly you tweak the comp plan, you'll start to stall (assuming no outright rebellion.) People may be upset, stop selling, and might even do bad things to you, like take their case to social media or online review boards, or take your people to another company.

Kody Bateman offers his thoughts about the risks of tinkering around during acceleration.

"The one thing you don't want to tweak too much is your compensation plan. You want to make the plan a part of your culture and stick with it. A change to the comp plan is the most difficult change to make in the field because people get very used to it.

"But there's a difference between a compensation plan and a marketing system. What I mean by tweaking is really the marketing system. What is the system that actually drives your compensation plan? Another way to ask that is: what is your duplicatable program? Some companies have a 90-day weight loss challenge and the challenge becomes the marketing system.

"And sometimes the marketing system needs to be tweaked a little bit—should it be 90 days or should it be 60 days? And the shift from 90 to 60 might be the key. Or should the fast start bonus be for bringing in five new customers or 10 new customers? Those are the things you have to mold and shape and tweak along the way."

Tread lightly whenever messing with compensation, product. or anything that affects the field's ability to *stay excited.*

BK Boreyko of Vemma spoke about the importance of taking the field into account when making any major changes.

"You've got so many things going on, so many moving pieces, that you need a core foundation for all your decisions. And for me, to this day, that foundation is: *how is this going to affect the field?*

"When I'm planning on doing something, I want feedback from the lead salespeople. If it's a change that affects the field, you need input from your leadership. They appreciate being involved in the process. The field leaders are your board of directors, so to speak. You can call them and say, 'What do you think about this?' Sometimes they'll say, 'Hey, that's great.' And sometimes they'll say, 'Are you crazy?' I think that's a critical part of the decision-making process. There are so many things that can go wrong, and you don't want to be the cause of that by making changes in isolation.

> You need a core foundation for all your decisions. And for me, to this day, that foundation is: how is this going to affect the field?

"Many times a company will make a decision or a policy change, and the change turns out to be a mistake. Then they have to either stick by it, so they're not embarrassed that they made a bad decision, or they change it and look like they don't have their acts together."

Kody Bateman emphasizes this point: "What puts a company into momentum in the acceleration phase is very delicate. A little tweak to your plan can either put you into acceleration or keep you from it. It's very, very sensitive. Once you find that spot where people are duplicating fast, they're excited about the plan, and they're acquiring momentum, you need to leave it alone. Let it percolate, and let it go. You have to give these programs time. A lot of companies tweak their plans when they don't get results in the first 30 days, and I think that's a mistake. You need to give your plan a strong 90 to 120 days in the marketplace to really formulate and gain momentum.

"This is a mistake I've made myself: the tendency to tweak your plan, your fast starts, your marketing systems a little bit faster than you should. Give it time to bake."

Several industry people I spoke with cautioned about adding products during acceleration.

BK says, "You've got to be careful about adding products. When you do that, people tend to stop and want to learn, when you want to keep them growing. When you do launch your product, you've got to be real precise so the downtime involved in learning about it doesn't take away from their ongoing recruiting or selling time.

"Sometimes people think a new product is the answer, and it's not always the case. They have to fit in with the mission. Is it something that will extend the market reach of your business? When you launch a new product, you want to be sure it will attract a bigger market share. So you just have to be careful."

Kimberly Cornwell of Celadon Road echoes this advice.

"You've got to be true to what you think your company is and what you want your ideal to be because that's what your consultants will respect. If you're constantly changing your product line and comp plan, or you're constantly morphing to try to be what the marketplace wants, I think you lose that credibility."

Although one should be careful about making adjustments during acceleration, there are times when changes are necessary. As you're accelerating, there's more pressure on all seams. People will be clamoring for solutions, which have to be viewed with caution, but there will undoubtedly be a need for new and better things to help the field build its business. It's just smart to be really thoughtful and cautious here.

ACCELERATION LESSON #10

Focus on Exactly What the Field Needs, But No More.

As you transition from launch into the acceleration period, the field needs to automate what they do so that it becomes easier to grow.

They're not always going to be able to get tender loving care from their up-line or from corporate, as the company has more and more people to deal with. And the more people they've got to deal with in the field, the more automated some of their tools are going to need to be, so they can be easily accessed and remove friction from building the business.

But a less obvious point to keep in mind is that what got you here won't get you there as you begin to build into growth. When you're moving from launch to acceleration, there's certainly a case to be made for changing up what you're doing. Maybe it's a brand refresh or maybe there are new tools you can develop.

One way to zero in on these needs is simply to ask the field. This means getting really close to the field leaders. The challenge is "shiny object" syndrome, where everyone's coming at you with, "We need this, we need that." Of course, you'll hear this all the way through the life cycle of your company, because you've got thousands of people with different opinions on what they need or what they had at their former company, etc.

It's super important for the corporate team to take a hard look at any new decisions, tools, systems, or changes that affect the field. They should consider such things from all sides You can chase that shiny new thing all the way into a hole, and waste the time, resources, and talent that are so scarce during acceleration.

ACCELERATION LESSON #11

Beware of Uncontrolled Growth.

While most companies would give anything to achieve stellar growth, growing too fast can come with a price.

As Dan Jensen told me, "Unfortunately, this kind of growth has often been a major cause of the demise of many otherwise successful ventures. Success is wonderful, but it can bury you. New businesses have new staff, new computer systems, new facilities, and are short on the experience to handle business efficiently. A home office can only handle a certain volume of business. What if that volume is exceeded? What if they run out of product for several weeks? Something must give.

"Growth can be very expensive. While growing, cash seems unlimited. Some growing companies go on a spending spree, throwing money at their problems. This too is a false security, for as surely as the growth came it will soon level out, and eventually go downward for periods of time. It may be far better to limit growth temporarily, than to succumb to its crushing demands."

Christy Prunier, the founder of pre-teen-focused direct seller WillaGirl, is aware of the risk of too much growth as a startup. "Something that I'm learning is that we can grow incredibly fast, but I've also learned about being deliberate with momentum because it has to be controlled. You don't want to grow too fast and then have to call back certain things that you've promised to your field, or without having the right systems in place. We want grow fast but smart and make sure that we're providing everything that our people need. And sometimes momentum requires slowing down in order to speed up."

Kody Bateman: "People who are new to the industry have this unrealistic expectation about how quickly they're going to grow. There are the anomalies, those companies that grow immediately and explode. But the majority of companies, if successful, have organic, progressive growth. And it takes a little longer than some realize to really grow that phase.

"It's not a one or two-year thing. It can take three or four years to be able to hit momentum you need and to gain trust, where consumers are going to say: 'I trust what they're about and I know they're going to be around.'

"The ones that grow at a reasonable pace have the staying power. Companies that crush it in their fourth or fifth year are normal in the industry. The plan should be to gain momentum in your fourth, fifth, and sixth years out."

Sometimes momentum requires slowing down in order to speed up.

Let's say one of those anomalies hits it big. How can a direct selling company control its growth? Dan Jensen offers the following options:

"Start locally by not accepting distributor applications from everywhere until you are ready. Distributors who seek to join from unopened regions can simply be given a courteous thank you letter and added to a list. Let them know how much you want to have them join, but that the opportunity isn't available yet in their area. Notify them when they can join. Don't sponsor road trips by corporate or field promoters. Take advantage of the less expensive local opportunities. Meetings can be held locally every night of the week for the cost of one meeting on the road. Don't recruit professional direct selling promoters or big hitters. If they want to join, then they must join as any other distributor.

"By controlling growth, a business plan can become a real guide to making the business profitable. Use the plan to make success become a reality and don't be too anxious to build your walls before you have built a solid foundation."

ACCELERATION LESSON #12

Avoid Near-Sightedness.

Companies can become myopic during acceleration. They tend to work on what's right in front of them. They will be narrowly focused on what they need to deliver right now, out of necessity. Projects that apparently seem less important fall to the wayside because everyone's so busy.

It's easy to lose sight of your strategy and greater vision when things are going good and growth is accelerating. The problem is that you don't see the forest for the trees because you're so close to everything. And when you look up, things are changing and you haven't planned for it. That's the danger of getting too focused on the day-to-day and not staying strategic. A good board of directors or a visionary CEO can help keep this in check.

It's important to have a strategic focus and plan, so that you know where the company is going one year, three years, and five years down the road. And not just in terms of results, but in terms of the general business climate and what's happening in the industry. All those things come into the mix. Strategic focus is the way to combat myopia.

"The field leadership's job is to focus on the next thirty days," says BK Boreyko. "But as corporate leaders, our job is to focus on the next six months, twelve months, twenty-four months. If you're doing that, you're doing your job."

ACCELERATION LESSON #13

Stay Connected With the Field.

When everything gets busy during acceleration, companies can start to lose touch with the field and with what's going on. This may be the most crucial time to stay connected and keep encouraging them. Social media is a vehicle you can use to stay in touch and maintain crucial relationships. Social media is really powerful in reaching out to people, thanking them, reaffirming them, and recognizing them, and it scales really well. It's still important to reach out to people with a phone call, to congratulate them for making rank, but when you've got thousands of people coming into the business, it's kind of difficult to do that in a manual way. Social then becomes your community, where the company can touch people much more effectively and frequently than almost any other type of communication.

Conversations through your social media platforms can give people the feeling that they're important and special. Leveraging such technology to do that is a really important concept.

In our firm's social media practice, the mantra is, "No post left behind!" Our goal is to make sure that every single person who reaches out to our client or posts a comment is engaged with and responded to in the right way. Companies should never leave that stuff untouched. If people are saying, "(Your Company), I'm so glad I joined you," and the company ignores them, it's almost like turning your back on them in person.

The social sphere can be a lonely place, and when the company or founder reaches out to them on their social channel, it can make their week a happy one.

When people are excited about joining, that's also a great opportunity to reach out to them and make them feel good about their decision. Validate their decision to work hard and make rank. Social media, done the right way, is immeasurable in its ability to make people feel important, listened to, and respected.

For Anna Zornosa of Ruby Ribbon, it's crucial to stay in close touch with the field both in social media and in person in order to anticipate their changing needs.

"During acceleration, we've started to see women get to the middle levels in the career plan and take on more responsibilities in managing their business communities. Today we have 2,000 women operating at the leader level or higher. One of the things that we think about now is how to transfer more responsibilities from company leadership to field leadership. We've anticipated that different levels on the career path have different needs from us.

"The company's full-time employees spend an awful lot of time traveling in the field. All of us expect to be out of the office at least a third of the time, attending meetings and making sure that women know our products, have a personal connection to the company, and realize they can become leaders. We invest a lot in events and training for them. Nothing radical, but our corporate team has a strong conviction that we're here to service them and that our time is best spent in the field."

ACCELERATION LESSON #14

Hire Experts to Fill the Gaps.

During acceleration, your internal team is going to be inundated with tasks and projects. It's hard to recruit the right people for the team at corporate while you're growing like that, because you're just so busy doing different things. This is true throughout the life of a direct selling company, but it's particularly crucial during acceleration when it's just grow, grow, grow. You've got events going on, you've got all sorts of big projects and expansion underway, lots of travel, lots of craziness. It's difficult to focus on bringing in the right team and ramping them up.

At this stage it might make sense to rely on outsiders who've shown expertise in certain areas. Hiring the right outsourcer for your inventory management might be a wise choice, or maybe a trainer to address a certain area that you need to focus on. Fortunately, just like for startup companies, there are plenty of experienced industry experts available to address any functional area of a more mature direct seller's business. The DSA does a great job of peer networking and educational content at its events, and its supplier members are top-notch.

Although a company's natural instinct may be to try to build everything internally, there's a wealth of resources out there, and it may makes sense to consider outsourcing during this stage of momentum.

Case Study: Southwestern Advantage Deals With a Crisis.

A classic example of expert crisis management occurred at Southwestern Advantage last year. The company trains college students to sell educational books door-to-door during the summer.

In 2013, a malicious rumor circulated over social media (reaching 38 million people, according to the company's estimate) that the company's salespeople, many of whom are exchange students from foreign countries, were suspected child abductors, human traffickers, or Russian spies (you read that right—Russian spies).

When I first heard this story at a DSA event, as a marketing professional, I was horrified. Their company was truly in a social media hellstorm. Horrible stories and accusations were being manufactured about them, and they could only sit and watch as it all went viral and continued to gain steam over weeks and weeks.

As disturbing as the event was, equally impressive was the company's response and dramatic turnaround. To counter the rumors, Southwestern launched a massive public awareness campaign via social media and over 150 other media outlets.

I asked Trey Campbell, Southwestern's Director of Communications who helped direct the company's response, to summarize the main principles direct sellers should keep in mind when they encounter a crisis.

"Number one, be prepared in advance and have a crisis plan along with action steps to take. Social media needs to be a part of that. What if a rumor starts? What if a representative goes rogue and makes false claims? You need not only a plan with actions steps, but you have to be clear on who's going to take those steps. Who will be the spokesperson for the company and how will that take place? A crisis takes on a life of its own and it's always something that you're not prepared for. Be as prepared as possible, because it's only a matter of time before something eventually happens to your company.

"Number two is transparency. Always be transparent about who you are, what you're doing, and the products that you represent. We've always done this and we've always taught this. We emphasize transparency in all of our training.

"Number three is to act quickly when a crisis occurs. Social media works at the speed of light and there's no stopping it. The old adage is that people usually have more negative than positive things to say, and that's true on social media as well. And we need to understand that we can't control it. But what can be controlled is the company's response when a problem arises. It's important to be proactive and preventative.

"And number four is to have empathy for the consumer. Put yourself in the shoes of the person you're talking to and try to relate to them. When you're trying build a relationship with someone, listening is key to understanding what their needs are. We tell the students: 'Don't sell them our product just to sell them our product. Sell them a product that they need.' And if you're doing that, chances are you won't run into problems."

Transparency is crucial to successful and ethical direct selling. As Kerry Brown of Crankshaft Marketing told me, people nowadays are more willing to forgive a company that isn't perfect, as long as the company engages honestly with their audience: "When they try to cover things up, then the field knows that they're putting up a corporate wall."

When problems arise, address them openly and honestly. If you ignore them or let them fester, you're headed for trouble.

A recent client launched successfully with a lot of excitement. However, due to complications with their software vendor, for the next *six weeks* they were unable to pay commissions and reward the hardworking reps who had gone out and sold for them. I first learned about this in a regular call with the CEO (who was new to the industry), who mentioned the issue in passing and asked, "What do you think?"

Alarmed at what I heard (and the CEO's apparent *lack* of alarm) I said: "You are now in a crisis. This is a company-defining moment for you. First, go get a calculator and figure out what those check amounts should be and who should get them. Then, you get in the car and go to the software vendor's office and sit on them until they fix the problem. Because your company's going to fail if you don't."

I was dead serious! This issue was choking the motivation out of the field by the minute. "They're not trusting that you'll pay them," I told him, "which is the biggest mistake you can make. They've talked about the business with their friends and family, and now they're sitting around waiting for a check that hasn't come in?

"The third thing you need to do is get out an email and tell the field exactly what the problem is, why it's happening, and what they can expect. Don't give them a deadline on when you're going to pay them because you don't know it at this point. Be honest and credible. Don't hide behind anything, just jump out in front of it and say, 'Here's the problem, you're my friend, I hope you understand we're starting up this company, I'm as sick about this as you are, I promise you'll get paid if I have to pay you myself.'

"And third: You get out that checkbook and start cutting checks by hand. You determine what each person is owed and you pay them out of your own personal bank account. It's that simple."

So that's what they did. By doing the above and being responsive, transparent, and accountable, the CEO was able to turn a potentially catastrophic event into a legendary credibility builder.

This is how we should address any crisis. It's too easy to get stuck in daily work mode, but if we're not on top of festering issues we could look up one day and find everything in chaos.

ACCELERATION LESSON #15

Don't Neglect Customer or Distributor Service.

Another difference between direct selling and mainstream businesses is that customer support is *really* important to our success. An airline can provide subpar service, but you still have to get somewhere. A retail clerk at a big box store can be inept but you'll still shop there if the prices are good.

In our business, support makes all the difference.

Christy Prunier of WillaGirl told me, "Priority number one is customer service and being able to compete with the Amazons of the world, where you can order today and have the product tomorrow. That kind of efficiency and customer service is paramount."

Dan Jensen reiterated this advice, with a focus on meeting the needs of distributors.

"One of your most critical departments is the one that handles problems, complaints, inquiries, and a thousand other issues that arise from your sales force. Your sales force is composed of volunteers and will quickly fire you if they are not well taken care of. Your distributor services department should consist of an elite 'SWAT' team with an obsession for excellence in customer service. They must be trained by those with a similar passion for excellence."

Because it is a cost center, this function can take a back seat to other, more revenue-driven areas of the business. It is too often an afterthought. Some companies even attempt to rely solely on the internet to provide support.

"Don't fall into this trap," Dan says. "Direct selling is a relationship business. Use the internet to take care of some of the needs of your sales force, but you can never build relationships and loyalty through the Internet. That takes person-to-person contact."

"Some direct selling companies find that their average distributor stays active only a few months, while for others it's several years. What's the difference between them? It's not the compensation plan. It's not the products they sell. Instead, it's how well the distributor is taken care of.

Terrel Transtrum of ServiceQuest says, "If your customer service people are doing poorly, the company will not be successful in the long run. If the distributors rave about the excellent service they receive, if they trust that their enrollees will be well taken care of, they'll recruit. If they have doubts that an enrollee would be happy, they'll hold back.

A customer service system must include the ability to track satisfaction levels. When a distributor phone call is logged and closed, a follow up call is placed, an email sent, or a survey letter mailed to the distributor asking: 'Was your call answered in a timely manner? Was the customer service representative courteous and professional? Was your question answered to your satisfaction?'

"Questions such as these, when answered by field distributors, become invaluable in reaching the goal of customer service excellence. The best software packages today incorporate customer service excellence systems to make excellence become a reality. Some companies provide bonuses to those reps who are consistently scored well by the distributors they serve."

ACCELERATION LESSON #16

Polish the Brand.

Up until the 1990s, direct selling companies did very little branding, and the little they did wasn't very good. They produced 30-minute fire-side chat videos featuring the founder explaining why the company was such a great opportunity. Little real marketing was done. The story went, "We don't spend money on branding or advertising because that money goes to the distributors."

In the 1990s, nutritional juice company Monavie decided to market their products differently from the past, with beautiful bottles, gorgeous pictures of their product splashing through water, and the like. Their modern (at the time) take on branding created a monster. The imagery created credibility for those who didn't identify with old scruffy MLM branding.

In the last ten years or so, direct sellers have morphed into strongly-branded companies that younger people would want to be associated with and to sell for. Today, branding for many direct sellers is on par with that of major retailers and mainstream companies, who spend millions on branding. Take Stella & Dot, Chloe & Isabel, or even the older companies Tupperware and Avon, who have rebranded to match current tastes. They show a connection with more modern sensibilities. As a result, today's generation doesn't identify at all with the baggage and general ickiness of the past. Branding and image enhancement have a lot to do with that, and the industry should be proud of its beautiful new era in branding, especially since it's now a crucial element in attracting younger people to the business.

Kerry Brown of Crankshaft Marketing offers the following about the importance of brand:

"The brand is the heart and soul of the company. It's just not a logo or a color or even a slogan or a tag line. A brand is a living, breathing organism that is your company.

"You want your field to be proud of that brand, and that takes work. It's not something that happens by accident. It takes planning. It's takes effort. It's not inexpensive. And those companies that have a strong brand have a much higher success ratio and even higher retention. People fall in love with more than just the product. Yes, they love the products and products are important. But they also fall in love with the brand itself and what it represents, and become part of something larger than themselves.

"Your brand has to be mobile friendly. The images and the message behind those images need to be easily shareable on Facebook, Twitter, and Instagram. A shot of the product in a testimonial doesn't work anymore. What's the product going to do for me and what's the opportunity for the potential new prospect? That message has to be in line with your brand."

I asked Kerry about voice and how that relates to social media.

"Voice is an often overlooked part of branding. The voice is how you speak to the field. How do you speak to your employees as well as to your prospects? Is it fun? Is it casual? Or is it formal and informative and educational? Is it a little bit flippant? Does it have a dab of arrogance and swagger? Or is it a soft sell, touching and familiar?

"Identifying the voice of the company and how that voice represents the company's messages is very critical. And all those elements go into the way that the brand is displayed in the media. Having cohesive brand strategies is first and foremost, and then developing the content and creative material to support that brand strategy.

"The entire strategy has to look like a well-orchestrated symphony. People will sniff out inconsistencies within your brand. If your message on Facebook doesn't line up with your YouTube videos or website, you can be viewed as not genuine. The brand is who you are, and when people see inconsistencies, you're seen in a bad light."

ACCELERATION LESSON #17

Once You Have the Right Brand, Do Everything You Can to Protect It.

The flip side of branding in the online world is that brands can be devalued or even hijacked, by both outsiders and even the field. Not only do you have the giant task of managing your brand competitively in the marketplace, you also have to manage the thousands of independent representatives who may have a different opinion about it, and use only parts of the brand, or none of it, when they sell your products. As you grow, you may find horrendous things being done to your brand—people using the name or logo in a way it shouldn't be used, or co-opting your brand to sell their own products and services. Over time, your brand equity begins to erode.

A major new development we see in our Reputation Defense practice is the rise of the "brandjacker" (a term our Scott Allen coined). Search the name of any major seller online today, and in most cases you'll find videos in the top 10 results from someone not related to the company that will say, "Is (Your Company) a scam? Click here and find out." So people will naturally click on the video, which might say something like this: "It's not a scam, but you should really learn about our sales system. Because if you're going to join X company, you need to use this sales system."

The last few years has seen a class of online marketers (actually, I shouldn't use the word "class" in the same sentence) who have found that they can reach the thousands of people you have worked tirelessly to bring to your front door, and then redirect them with savvy yet questionable marketing practices away from your opportunity and to their crappy sales system or "leads" lists.

Make no mistake, these bottom-feeders are competing directly with you for the consumer's attention and dollars. Once the user clicks to the video or website, who knows where they'll end up? But the risk that you'll lose them has just increased significantly.

80% of the top 100 direct sellers' search results feature a prominent brandjacker enjoying the results of all the traffic our companies worked so hard to nurture.

Why are brandjackers so easily able to get into the top 10 search results for your brand name? Because few direct sellers have invested in protecting their names with strong reputation defense practices. Frankly, it's easy to ride the coattails of a company that hasn't protected its brand.

In a recent study we did at our firm, we found that nearly 80% of the top 100 direct sellers' search results feature a prominent brandjacker enjoying the results of all the traffic our companies worked so hard to nurture.

Brandjackers are very difficult to remove from your search results because they are so prolific. They're a real problem, and almost unique to our industry. At our firm we're now deep into our own research about how to combat them and what kinds of programs we can put in place to defend the industry against them. Not only are they siphoning off people we've worked hard to attract to our businesses, but they're using the word "scam" and that scares people off. We're used to it in this industry, but everyday people are not, and it is a powerful repellent to new people joining up.

Brandjacking is something you have to prepare for well in advance. If you're starting a company, you need to strengthen the search pages so that brandjackers can't get in so easily.

As I write this, I'm on a plane leaving a new client who has not yet even chosen their name. They were surprised when I underscored the importance of carefully choosing the brand name based not entirely on marketability or domain name availability, but also on the potential for negativity, search power, and ease of strengthening in their future search results. I told them that as soon as they become successful, the target will be on their back, the brandjackers will converge on their brand, so the decisions they make now will determine what they'll need to fix later.

So how do you protect your name, the names of the founders, and your products online? By deploying a name protection program as far in advance as possible. You can help keep your Google results clean and prevent brandjackers from easily popping in by building strength on the links to friendly and neutral web properties via backlinks, maintaining a robust social media presence, having well-clicked and viewed YouTube videos, using GooglePlus, and employing other natural methods to provide search strength (or "Google juice"). It's not easy, it takes experience, time and money to get right, but it's absolutely worth it.

ACCELERATION LESSON #18

Advertising Is No Longer Optional.

For a hundred years it's been against the grain in our industry to advertise. We pass the savings to the consultants, right? It's also been a clear channel conflict in that the field won't benefit from money spent on ads made for the company, at least not directly.

Even the company website has traditionally been viewed as a conflict with the field's replicated websites. Today there are still direct sales companies that require the visitor to enter the distributor's name and ID number before they can order product from the company website. In the past, this made sense, as a smart company doesn't want to appear to compete with its field.

Of course, advertising has changed, and these days to compete you have to advertise to some extent. Maybe not in TV commercials, but in other ways.

Facebook, for example, has been a boon to direct sellers for several years now. But now that Facebook is a public company they have their own quarterly numbers to hit. You'll now need to pay them if you expect your content to be widely seen. As soon as we learned this at our firm, we instituted a pay-for-play strategy and added a budget for our clients meant to ensure the delivery of the content we develop for them. It's the new reality, and if you are not boosting your content on Facebook it is less likely to ever be acted upon or even seen.

Keep in mind your content still needs to be excellent so you'll still need the same (or better) level of management of your platform because you still need people clicking through and becoming interested in what you have to say.

We also recommend to our clients to buy all their branded terms on Google via Adwords. This is good for your search results, in that if someone looks you up in a hurry, it's worth the buck or two to have them click directly on your paid link, rather than scroll down and happen upon a brandjacker or Scam.com.

ACCELERATION LESSON #19

Embrace New Media, Technology, and Change.

BK Boreyko, known in the industry as a leader in the change department, particularly in technology and sales innovations, recently made some changes to Vemma's compensation plan that essentially switched the company to a more affiliate-based model (defined as one or two levels of pay.) The move, considered bold if not somewhat controversial, is being watched closely by the industry.

"I don't think the industry changes fast enough," BK says. "I think it's so entrenched in how it has done business, in what has got them to where they are, that I don't think they understand that they're going to need to do some things completely differently to get to where they want to go. I don't know if I'm the best guy to say how the industry is changing, because I don't really see much changing. It's pretty much doing business the way it did five and ten years ago.

"Companies incorporate technology, which is fine. But that's not really change; they're not the ones up there leading the way. They're out there adapting to what is happening."

Ivy Hall of Initials, Inc. sees changes in the direct selling landscape.

"The entire marketplace has really reshaped over the nine years we've been in business. It has been a constant evolution of watching trends, watching how people communicate and connect, and creating opportunities to stay on top of that.

"The new tool of connecting for our generation has been social media. But it's also what direct selling has been doing for over a hundred years—sharing with friends. It's in women's DNA to want to share, and social media is a tool that allows that to happen quickly and effectively.

"Social media has not only influenced how we're shifting our outbound message but also how we communicate with our field. People respond more to an image or a video than they do to the written word. And so we've stepped back and asked ourselves: how are we communicating? We review the analytics to see what people are watching or viewing. And we've changed, as much as we can, to communicate more with images.

"Communicating new product releases and promotions requires bullets, images, and video. And then outbound, we're using social media to connect. People go to a company's website for information, but we're finding just as many people are going to Facebook. The website is what we're saying about ourselves, but our social media is showing not only what we're putting out about ourselves, but how others are responding and sharing that information."

It's in women's DNA to want to share, and social media is a tool that allows that to happen quickly and effectively.

Kody Bateman of SendOutCards also emphasizes the need for direct sellers to embrace the fundamental changes that are taking place.

"There are a lot of people in the industry who still believe in the old school of belly-to-belly, face-to-face communication as the primary model that works. It has worked for 50 years in this profession, and is a cornerstone of what we do for a living. But like it or not, it's changing dramatically.

I think direct selling people need to embrace social media much, much more. The big mistake is for people to think that they can build their companies the same way Uncle Joe did 20 years ago."

Kody admits that it was a bit of a stretch for him to adapt. "To be honest with you, I was kind of late to social media. I'm a traditional guy and I like the old school way. It took me longer than I'm willing to admit to really dramatically make the shift and realize that social media practices have to be mainstream in building a business—mainstream in how you prospect; mainstream in how you present your products to people, and mainstream in follow-up and training. We need to embrace that."

I asked Kody how his company is using technology and social media to build and sustain momentum in his company.

"We do greeting cards and gifts, and our product is purchased 100% online. The whole user experience is online—you custom-build the greeting card and push the send button, which delivers it to our fulfillment service, where the card is printed, stamped, and mailed. So our approach is a bit unique compared to other direct sales companies. We're utilizing a Pinterest-style sharing platform.

"And we're planning to debut some really cool technologies this year. We will add our own Pinterest-style board where people can share card ideas and send cards. Let's say a real estate agent wants to reach his customers six or seven times a year. Instead of sending a single card a year, he wants a campaign. He can go on this platform and look at the ideas of other real estate agents who have card campaigns. He can glean information from those campaigns and even share the cards. So this is just one example of how we're leapfrogging over current technologies. It's very, very exciting."

ACCELERATION LESSON #20

Make it Shareable.

Anna Zornosa of Ruby Ribbon explores effective ways of reaching the field and the public through social media.

"Our stylists don't all want to hear from us every day. It's overwhelming. On the other hand, the leader has a huge appetite for communication, and needs to have different and additional ways to get that information in a timely way. We use social media a lot for that.

"Last year at this time, we had meetings just for upcoming leaders. Right now we're simultaneously planning for our first stylist meeting and our first director level meeting. So all of a sudden we really have to be thinking on two fronts, not about just a growing national network of stylists, but about our expectations for different groups of women, including leaders who are building teams of their own."

Anna understands that what is interesting gets shared. And when it's shared, it exponentially increases the reach of your message to new people.

"We program social media a lot more. Every week we feature six or seven types of clothing on Facebook, things that are branded and have an interesting look, so it encourages our stylists to share them. It's not uncommon for clothes to have 60 or 70 shares. And on days when we have a post that 60 or 70 stylists are sharing on their own pages, we'll get a whole lot more. It's very deliberate and thoughtful programming that delights the stylists so much that they want to post it on their own pages."

Kimberly Cornwell of Celadon Road elaborates on her company's use of Facebook parties.

"We're training our consultants to think outside the box in utilizing social networks in advantageous ways, that will not be off-putting to their friends or extended networks. That includes showing them how to do a Facebook party that's fun and will draw people in, as opposed to making people feel they were pulled in. We tell the consultants, *Make it fun. Picture yourself in the mud mask. Get your customers talking and excited about what you're doing.*

"We're finding a lot of traction on Twitter. We're also going to be launching a mobile app with a new partner. We're just trying to think outside the box.

"Our virtual parties have been increasing dramatically. We're doing in-person parties and also catalog parties, so a woman who doesn't want to have a party at her home can show the catalog to her friends. But now, with the way our software works, each of those two parties can also have an online component. We've merged components so that our consultants can add a virtual party to their existing in-person party."

Kimberly reveals the challenges of holding a virtual party versus a real one.

"Ensuring consumer engagement is a challenge. Maybe 25 people will be interested in a virtual party, but only five show up. And those who do will still drop in and out because they get distracted by other things going on in social media."

> The younger consultants and the younger customers are completely fine with totally virtual. Some in their 20s have never done in-person parties, only virtual.

So the key, Kimberly says, is to hook them early: "Keeping their attention is what we're trying to get our consultants to do, perhaps through showing a mini-video. Our consultants have found is that it's best not to shop while the party is on. Just have fun and talk about the company, and then people can go and shop online. You're not looking somebody in the eye and holding their attention, so you have to find ways to get them interested virtually. If you don't have them hooked in 2.6 seconds, they're looking to leave the party.

"I don't think virtual parties will become our primary way of holding parties, but every day it becomes a larger component of our business. The younger consultants and the younger customers are completely fine with totally virtual. Some in their 20s have never done in-person parties, only virtual. They're completely fine with it, while women in their 30s and 40s prefer that personal contact."

ACCELERATION LESSON #21

Social Media is Not a Panacea.

By now you may have the impression that I'm a fan of social media. (You'd be right!)

But I also understand its limits.

Social media doesn't substitute for the tried and true methods our industry has always used to attract customers and sell products. And that's because, in the end, it's all about relationships. It's more than mere transactions. If I call you up out of the blue and try to sell you something, it's not going to work. Direct selling is about getting to know someone. And once I get to know you, then I can inform or notify you about something. Social media works the exact same way and provides another avenue for building relationships.

"We have our sleepless nights over this question," says Andy Smith, General Manager of Amway UK. "I've been in direct sales for 31 years. I've been in the business my whole career with different companies. My kids are 19 and 21 now. They tell me they don't use Facebook anymore because I'm using Facebook, so that's not sexy anymore. Some of the technologies, particularly on social media, that we think are connecting with the younger generation, they're switching off. In some respects, younger people are going back to some of the old-fashioned principles of direct selling. The younger generation, they're meeting up. They use social media to meet face-to-face.

"I think we in some respects went too far across the spectrum to digital. We stopped printing recognition materials because we were trying to get out of print. I said to the marketing folks in the business, wait a minute, there's nothing more powerful than a handwritten postcard or a note that says, 'Congratulations, you've just achieved something this month.' Everything's email, but people have stopped reading emails; they've stopped reading online bulletins.

"We're going back into print on a lot of this stuff, trying to find a balance between high touch, the old personal touch, and digital. There's a danger of trying to be too fancy and expecting everybody to go digital. We're going back to bigger meetings and conferences that might seem old-fashioned. Direct selling is a community, and there's a danger of losing the community spirit by having everything online."

As exciting and new as social media is for networking and sharing, we should always focus on the ultimate connection, as there is a hierarchy to building relationships.

Richard Brooke speaks about both the limitations and tremendous opportunities presented by social media.

"The analogy I like to make is this: emailing somebody about your product as a direct seller is like emailing someone your romantic intentions. Getting a prospect on the telephone vs. email is a quantum leap in the connection that you make. If you're not clear about it, imagine that you emailed someone romantically and then finally got on the phone with them. It's a quantum leap in the connection. And the next quantum leap is to go on Skype to see them. But nothing compares to actually being in their presence. Nothing substitutes for that we-had-coffee-last-week, or I-was-at-your-house-and-met-your-kids connection.

"And that's what we have to fight to hang on to. In the new age of direct selling, we have to continually figure out ways to maximize technology to extend our reach and increase our efficiencies, and still be a able to wrap our arms around our marketplace and give 'em a big hug. Nothing compares to that."

Richard is optimistic but pragmatic about technology strengthening or complementing those relationships.

"Social media is a fantastic efficiency tool that I would never want to give back. In the physical realm, you're limited by time and space. But in the technical realm, you have a leap in efficiencies because you're not limited by anything. What we have to do is keep the classic high tech/high touch thing in balance, so that as we gain efficiencies in high tech, we also continue to aggressively create opportunities for high touch. We don't want the technology to outstrip us."

Rob Snyder of Stream Energy has a similar view.

In the new age of direct selling, we have to continually figure out ways to maximize technology and still be a able to wrap our arms around our marketplace and give 'em a big hug. Nothing compares to that.

"I don't think you can build your business on social media alone. Social media will be most effective in circumstances where someone already has an existing relationship with a person. Social media can serve as a kind of a bridge in that regard, when two people can't meet because of physical distance or other barriers. Social media complements the person-to-person connection. As people become increasingly comfortable with social media, they will learn how to use it more effectively."

Jan Gilmore believes that social media has enormous advantages, but it also has a number of disadvantages if it's not used properly.

"Once upon a time, at least 50% to 60% of the people who joined your company would actually do something from the beginning. Today that's closer to 25%, particularly in the party plan.

"Today, people sign up online more than they sign up through person-to-person contact. Suddenly you're part of my company, but I don't know anything about you. And because people join so easily, they take it a little bit for granted. Years ago in the party plan situation no one joined until you met them, explained it to them, showed them the contract, and signed it, together. You established a relationship. Today that doesn't happen as much. And that's a problem, because if people can join so easily, they can also leave easily. There's less care and nurturing in the relationship today.

"Too many people believe that if they can tweet and use Instagram, they're in business. Some companies are becoming more aware of that and are trying to be proactive in teaching people how to effectively use social media. Social media greatly widens your sphere of influence, but it doesn't substitute for the hard work of building relationships.

Jan warns against the dangers of complacency. "One company I'm working with now communicates entirely through Facebook, instead of calling the hostess two or three times and spending time getting to know her before the party, to make sure everything's on track. If you never speak to the hostess, have no relationship with her, and she doesn't have to report back to you verbally, you might be disappointed when you get to the party and find only four people there. Connecting with people 24/7 is very important today, but it has to be done with that old sense of building and nurturing relationships."

Finally, Seth Godin, bestselling author and marketing guru once wrote about the network marketing model and the ease by which social media can propel it, and often not in a positive way. He said, "We're hardwired to respect real authenticity, and at some level, that means trusting the motives of the person we're listening to. The bottom line is, just because the net makes it much easier to measure things, share things, create downlines and hierarchies and yes, scams, doesn't mean its the best way to make something that lasts."

My thoughts exactly. Our focus should always be on relationships, not just clicks.

Case Study: Careful Raising Walls in Social Media.

With all the marketing power of social media, there's an equally beneficial use for it: community. But sometimes social media marketing and community are mutually exclusive.

We had a social media client recently who had, prior to our starting with them, set up a Facebook group for their field. Groups can be a good way to connect and build relationships between people already in the group. Groups, by nature, are more chatty. Posts are more viewable than on a page and are read more often, because members are notified of updates.

But there are very good reasons not to sponsor or encourage groups. As much as we love groups, the primary drawback is *they are not public.* All that fun and engagement is completely lost on your marketing efforts, and the activity in groups can effectively "cannibalize" your Facebook page activity.

Our advice to our client was to wean the field off the group and focus on the public page. They were not experiencing the growth they wanted on Facebook despite great content and other significant advantages.

If you must sponsor a group, we suggest making it exclusive to the upper ranks. That's where you want to foster community the most, and it's a nice reward for lower ranks to move up. Several of our clients have even been successful with company-sponsored "leader-only" groups to encourage collaboration at the top levels. However, monitoring this can be a full time job and a management headache.

Sadly, our client prefers to continue to promote the group (against our advice) and it continues to grow and grow in significance, while the company has not experienced the growth they surely would otherwise.

If you plan to focus on groups as a primary field tool, prepare for lower Facebook page growth and for your creative efforts to get far fewer views and shares from the people you most want to engage—your field *and their friends.*

ACCELERATION LESSON #22

Enhance the Event with Online Excitement.

I think most executives would agree that the live event cannot be replaced by technology, at least for the time being. But technology certainly has its place and can do wonders for your events.

The most obvious application is leveraging the field to promote events to their channels. Imagine if every attendee at a your annual conference were to check-in on Facebook and FourSquare when they arrived. During the sessions they "live tweet" the many interesting motivational quotes and quips heard from the stage. At the party that night, they share a ton of photos of all the fun they're having with their bored friends at home. YoutTube videos from the conference follow and lots of excited recaps in Facebook posts. What would this do for your company?

With hashtags, texts, social updates, and image sharing, you can keep the conversation going before, during, and after the sessions.

And if you really want to be successful as an energetic, multi-faceted direct selling company, extend your events with technology. Do it right, and the people who can't attend in person can be there virtually. People who don't know about the company can learn about it. All of this leads to your message being shared far beyond the ballroom walls. It's almost as if these technologies were made to do this very thing.

This is a good example of leveraging technology to *enhance* a critical function of our business, not replace it.

ACCELERATION LESSON #23

Educate the Field in the Limits to Technology.

If you're working inside a direct seller, you've no doubt noticed the increasing tendency for the field to do more and more their business online. The result is a proliferation of primarily online companies and affiliate-type models entering to meet the demand. A growing portion of networkers can build a business from their home in bathrobes, and not necessarily have the desire or need to use traditional network marketing methods. They use social media, write blogs, use the online world, and don't reach out much, if ever, via phone.

Relationships can't be replaced by a sales funnel in an online marketing environment. Social media can enhance the relationships that you have, and it can help you scale and reach people you might not otherwise have reached. Social media can help you identify yourself in the marketplace and inform the masses about what you do. But for most companies to sell and be successful, there's still a need for personal interaction. After all, it's what differentiates us from impersonal online retail and affiliate marketing models.

So the question is: how do we as an industry adapt and be as completely technologically proficient as we can, without sacrificing what makes us special in the first place?

We need to train and educate the field and utilize selling systems that encourage all the things that need to be done to be successful

ACCELERATION LESSON #24

Engagement is the Name of the Game.

The way we stay connected is through engagement. Engagement breeds interaction, and interaction is necessary because the social networks all have a built-in bias toward content that is acted upon. It is core to the way they work.

When you don't engage or engage poorly in social media, you are not only ineffective but penalized. Facebook, for example, uses its algorithm (known as "EdgeRank") to hide content it deems non-relevant from its users. A main component of that algorithm rests on interactivity. If your updates and photos do not induce commenting, liking, and sharing, they are much less likely to ever be seen at all.

Unfortunately, most direct sellers do not do a proper job of engaging and creating compelling content on their social sites. As a result, they fail to connect with their audience, which leads to dullness, poor results, and ultimately frustration. Some of you may have experienced this in your initial forays in social, where it just didn't work.

The average Facebook user spends 18 minutes on each site visit, creating 90 pieces of content. Multiply that by a billion and

a half users sharing 5 billion pieces of content daily with 130 friends each, and you'll soon realize how crowded and active it really is. New content must be *constantly* developed, and it has to be compelling enough to prompt sharing and further discussion.

The social network is a content-hungry beast. It eats everything in sight and still wants more. It's never satisfied. You need to feed it constantly with status updates, new videos, photos of your field having fun and making money, and all sorts of other content.

Not only do you need to stay active, you've got to have the right people managing all this. This is where the vast majority of companies start wrong. They ask the receptionist or marketing coordinator to "post and tweet" on top of everything else they're doing. Would you ask the junior bookkeeper to pretend to be CFO for part of the day?

In this new world we're in, social media is as important as any other function of your company. If your team doesn't have expertise in online community management, it'll show and your performance will be mediocre at best. You need people who understand social media deeply, and people who understand direct selling deeply.

Ours is not like other forms of business. Our communities are very different than those of a gift store or a burger chain. Networkers are much more "a part" of our brands than merely consumers. We know this. Our fans and followers interact differently and have different needs and wants. Whoever's at the controls must be skilled both in social media *and* direct selling.

ACCELERATION LESSON #25

Rock Out on All Social Channels.

I recently read in an direct selling industry magazine that a direct selling company really only needs to be good at one or two social media sites, an assertion I completely disagree with.

Why? Because you are turning your back on people who on the sites that you've chosen not to manage. My wife, for example, is not a huge fan of Facebook, but she really enjoys Pinterest. If you decide only to focus on Facebook and Twitter, you'll completely miss reaching this stay-at-home mom, a woman directly in one of the most sought-after demographics, and potentially *all her followers*. Lame.

Our position is you have to absolutely rock out all your platforms. That includes Facebook, Twitter, Pinterest, YouTube, LinkedIn, GooglePlus (yes), Instagram, and a field-focused blog. If you're going to commit, why just half-ass it?

The future audience you want—young, connected, and chatty—is on Twitter, Instagram, and SMS. Ignore a platform they love and your reach to them exponentially drops.

Rob Snyder reveals Stream Energy's move toward social media and mobile, to capitalize on this trend.

"In the last two or three months, we have declared to our field two things. First, we're moving heavily to social media to help propagate our message. But as the ease of social media rises, there's also an increase in white noise on social media. So it's important for us to provide our associates with effective marketing materials that will cut through that white noise and stand out.

"Second, the world is increasingly moving to the smartphone and we are as well. And the marketing tools we are developing for our team will be designed with a phone architecture in mind, not necessarily for implementation on a PC or a tablet."

Christy Prunier of WillaGirl talks about the need for further innovation in technology to help direct selling.

"Frankly, I don't think the technology is there yet. The platform where our girls spend the majority of their time is Instagram. And that platform isn't set up or monetized so a girl can have her own business there. We want to make sure that our brand is really working with girls in the way that they live. We're focusing on how we might use technology to make the experience of building her own business work on social media platforms."

Richard Brooke notes how quickly social media changes.

"Direct selling companies need to pay attention to how people in various demographics communicate. I'm 59 years old and two or three years ago I figured I ought to get on Facebook. Facebook is kind of a hip thing for me, but for teenagers it might as well be a rotary phone. And that will continue to change. Different demographics are going to have different favorite tools for communicating. And those tools will continue to be invented and created and promoted. Right now it seems to be Instagram, but what will it be three years from now?"

Now, how does that apply to your business? Do you have events? Perhaps your audience will "live tweet" during your events and share with all their friends. Do you have visitors to HQ? They may be checking in on Facebook or FourSquare and sharing their fun with everyone they know. What if everyone who went to a home party checked in on their social networks? How many people would that reach?

When you think about it, almost anything you do at your company has a sharable context to it.

So these super connected Millennials are the future of your company. And what do they want? Need? Crave?

Excitement!

Case Study: Busting the Top 6 Facebook Myths

Wonder why your company's Facebook page isn't performing as well as it could be? Hard to know. Direct selling companies all have different ideas about what will "work" on Facebook and misconceptions abound. Here are six myths to be aware of:

MYTH 1: "The More Posts the Better!" On Facebook, frequent posting does NOT equal success. The irony is, the more you post, the more your engagement is diluted and the less you'll be able to reach your audience. Posting too many messages per day can become bothersome to your fans—at best they will tolerate it, and at worst they will unsubscribe. Around here we call it "post fatigue."

Direct Sellers especially fall in this trap. We often use Facebook because we really want people to know about our company or opportunity. But overpost and you'll lose people. Take a close look at some of the larger direct sellers and you'll see a moderate amount of posting, even with huge fan bases. Stella & Dot, even with nearly 400,000 likers, still only post once or twice a day and even sometimes (gasp!) skip a weekend.

Solution?: We recommend—at most—one or two posts per day. Anything more borders on greedy. Reign in the frequency and spend that extra time on being more creative; you'll create better content, which is more important.

MYTH 2: "Facebook Should Be Treated Same As Our Website." I often find executives tend to treat social media as they would a web site. They craft and hone and polish and agonize over colors, images and pixels. Most are GenX'ers or Boomers who struggle to fully embrace the authentic, fast and "in the stream" nature of social media. Social media does not require perfection! In fact the more polished it is the less "real" it may seem. Overproducing social posts not only wastes your time, the polishing itself leads to less creative and genuine messaging, therefore less success overall.

Solution?: It's social media—just roll with it!

MYTH 3: "Facebook—It's The New Email!" Because our industry has relied so heavily on email, open rates these days are scary-low. So the tendency is to push on other channels to get the numbers up. But using Facebook like email will actually work against people ever seeing it. It's the way the algorithm works — purely informational posts get cut out of the news feed; too many will ding your newsfeed ranking. Facebook itself relieves the user of ever having to see boring posts because it knows what they want to see—and they don't want to see that 15th post about your next event.

Solution?: Don't inform, engage! Save email announcements for email.

Myth 4: "We should name the company, founder, product or event in every post!" Since most of your fans of the page are likely already distributors or customers, it's probably not necessary to add full names of your execs, founders, or company in each post. Since the user is visiting your page, they are probably aware of who is being represented by the page, right? If they want to know more they will click on "About."

Solution?: Keep your posts relevant, concise and interesting. Try to avoid starting out with "Here at ABC Company, we…" or "Our Founder and CEO, Ima D. Bigwig says…" Too long.

Myth 5: "Facebook is fine for longer posts." This is a biggie. Although Facebook posts have no obvious limit like Twitter's famous 140 characters, there is a practical limit for Facebook posts, about 200 characters. Social media is fast-moving stream and long posts will be rejected more often. Requiring the user to read too much reduces your effective engagement and disrupts the casual reader who, in many cases, is exactly who you're trying to reach.

Solution?: It's easy to know when you've hit the limit: If a finished post requires the user to click "See More" — it's too long.

Myth 6: "There's no way to know whether posts are good or bad." Some execs complain that Facebook is "mushy" and hard to quantify. Most aren't aware they can immediately assess the effectiveness of their program at any time by reviewing the visitor data.

Solution?: Data rules! It's all right there. Look to see what content is working, and do more of that. If your content doesn't get shared or liked, change it!

For a truly successful Facebook campaign, make sure your posts are unique, interesting, and engaging. Mix it up. Boost engagement with images and links. Most of all, make it *fun.*

ACCELERATION LESSON #26

Don't Be Boring.

To fulfill our destiny, we need to be exciting and compelling. So *don't be boring.*

Being boring is a no-no in social media. This includes posting boring things nobody cares about, repeating content, not posting enough, posting too much, not leveraging videos or photos, and just being uninteresting.

Sales messages are *especially* boring. People use social media to *share, learn* and *have fun.* They are not there to buy things. That doesn't mean they *won't* buy, but that's not why they visit.

Let's say you have a newbie distributor who signs up and likes your page. Then she gets constant boring updates crowding her newsfeed. She doesn't want to hide you because she's part of your brand, but she could be slowly turning off to the business, post by post.

Constant updates about your latest product, promotion, or event will turn off otherwise eager fans. Just as people can instantly "like" you, they can also instantly "hide" you and your posts forever. "Unsubscribe" and "unfollow" are one click away.

Social media is about excitement—*and so is this business!* If the things you're posting will not foster an interesting discussion, re-consider posting them. Before posting anything, as yourself: *will this annoy people enough to hide us?*

Part of not being annoying or boring is resisting the internal pressure to sell on social media.

Social media is not an advertising medium or a place to announce every little thing. Posts about the big fall promotion or an upcoming event can get boring fast, *especially* when repeated. We need to redefine our ideas about communicating with the field.

The word "communication" comes from the Latin "communico," meaning "share." This is what I love about social media—it enables the truest form of communication, *sharing*, on a massive scale.

In that respect, you can see what social media *is not*—it's not a press release launcher, or a promotional brochure, or even a website. It's a platform for interaction. It's dialogue rather than monologue. More cocktail party than broadcast booth.

Our industry, naturally, is a highly driven sales culture. It's what we do. So we have to be really vigilant in resisting the temptation to flood the social web with our sales stuff. Social media is not about us. It's about the field and the customers.

Do everything in your power to prevent your blog or fan page or twitter from being viewed internally as another way to "get the word out" about sales-driven topics.

If you need to advertise, buy ads. You don't want your precious fanbase to be viewed internally as a marketing list. It doesn't convert like that, and if you abuse it you'll lose the trust you worked so hard to build.

ACCELERATION LESSON #27

Leverage the Data.

How many direct sales companies have an absolute grasp on the demographics and psychographics of their fields? Not many. In the past, most companies gathered only the minimal amount of data. Maybe they had an address and zip code (which is really ridiculous when you consider we are in the sales and marketing business.)

An oft-overlooked side benefit to a robust social media program is the sheer amount of actionable data you will enjoy. Social media can provide you with amazing data and information about your field. The analytics you'll get from having a strong program will be immeasurably valuable to you.

A strong social media program also includes lots of listening, not only to your own social stream, but also across the social sphere to find out how people are discussing you. Set up a listening program. You will find this incredibly eye opening.

ACCELERATION LESSON #28

Train the Field to Use Social Media Responsibly.

"The single biggest momentum killer I see," Kody Bateman tells me, "is that a lot of reps don't realize the impact of what they post on social media. Social media has been the biggest opportunity for us. It's also been the biggest challenge for us as executives, because it moves so rapidly and everything is public. Any complaint is public. Any opinion is public. And reps have the tendency to go straight to social media with their opinions and complaints.

"Let's say that I started a direct sales business and I've been in it for 90 days. I haven't advanced in rank or made my first thousand dollars yet. But a few other people have, and they've also been in it for 90 days. Typical scenario, right?

"So I'm going to do one or two things. I'll try to figure out what I'm doing wrong and do it right. Or I'll try to figure out what's wrong with the system because it can't be my fault. It has to be somebody else's fault. So I get on social media and start to intentionally search for other people who are struggling and have complaints. And when I find a complaint, I'll latch on to it: *You know, $149 for a starter kit is too much. They should be $99* *instead. That's why I can't hit the numbers, 'cause you guys got the pricing screwed up.*

"The thread starts and the negativity spreads. That's a momentum killer not only for reps but for the company as a whole. The executives and reps in this industry need to do a much better job in teaching each other the importance of using social media for the right reasons. Always use social media to build up what you're doing, not to tear it down. If you want momentum, you have to be smart about gaining momentum. It's fine to have problems and complaints. But don't be public with them, because you'll kill momentum. We need to do a better job of teaching that fact."

ACCELERATION LESSON #29

Find Beauty in the Bumps

Direct selling is a very emotional business, and I think we need to acknowledge and embrace that, the ups and the downs, the joys and the sorrows.

It's very joyful because we get close to people and we can help them change their lives. If you really love people, it's a great industry. You know what our conventions are like.

They're like revivals. The first one I went to had upwards of 8,000 people in a basketball arena. When the company executives got on the stage, people were screaming like it was the end of the Earth. If you have a convention where everybody's just screaming and holding up placards, you've done a great job. You've got them excited about changing their lives and about building their businesses. And many of them are coming up from nothing, becoming somebody they never thought they would be.

But it's not an easy industry by any means. We all know the difficulties and the down times. And I think we can find sustenance and support in each other's struggles and triumphs. Certainly I felt that way when I spoke with Ivy Hall of Initials, Inc.

"Britney Vickery and I started the company out of a spare bedroom, so it wasn't like we had an incredible infusion of venture capital or something like that. I was seven and a half months pregnant the day that we launched, which, looking back, is completely insane.

"So there was a learning curve for us, being new to the industry. And one important thing I learned is that there's beauty in the bumps. In direct selling, a lot of times it's going to be hard. You're going to hit an obstacle and say to yourself, *Wow, I really, really messed up on that one* or, *that sure didn't turn out the way I planned.* There's always an opportunity for personal growth, corporate growth, and professional growth. And that growth takes place when you shift the mindset from the bump being something awful you have to climb over, to something beautiful you can learn from. That's when step you outside of where you are. That's when you advance and learn. And that's something we've really embraced as a company, to really savor the bumps, learn from them, and keep going.

"The night we launched the company the doorbell rang. It was a friend of mine and she said, *I can't come tonight, but I've been thinking about it and I want to be your first consultant.* And we said: *Really? Oh, fantastic!* She filled out the information, she handed us a credit card, and Britney and I looked at each other, high-fived, and hugged. We were officially in business. Then my friend walked out the door, and Britney and I looked at each other and said: *We have to figure out how to take credit cards.*

"Today, the challenges are a little more complex. We think a lot about how to create a company that's giving back. We've created a foundation and our goal this year is to fully fund ten adoptions. Where we are today is really different from where we were then. But it doesn't change how you approach challenge. It can either build you up or break you. So we've chosen the mantra that it's going to build us up and we'll grow from it."

***

So now you have an overview of the best practices to employ in accelerating through the atmosphere and escaping gravity. Your goal is to reach orbit, where you can sustain momentum for years to come. But orbit, too, has its own set of challenges and opportunities. In the last part of this book, we'll look at additional ways to maintain your speed in orbit and not come crashing back to Earth.

PART THREE

Reaching Orbit and Beyond.

You've accelerated and used up most of your fuel, and you've pierced the atmosphere. Now you're in orbit, you're successful, and things are going well. You've got an excited field, you've got volume, you've got people making money, your events are well attended, and you're growing at a good rate. Not a fantastic rate, but at a steady, sustainable rate.

The mature phase, like launch and acceleration, carries its own set of problems and challenges. Mature companies may become stalled because in any industry, market expansion is going to eventually hit a plateau. Eventually you're going to get pulled back to Earth, and at some point additional growth should come from finding new products or new markets.

Mature companies also stall because they're stuck in old business models or stale approaches. Throughout the ecommerce boom and many changes in the economy, direct sellers have kept plowing forward, thinking things will just take care of themselves. For the most part, they've been right. But old-line companies have realized this doesn't hold true anymore and are changing things up.

We have to adapt to the new world we're in. The industry has gotten by for a long time by doing the same thing again and again. And there's some truth about what we've always done, because it's worked. But if we look around us right now, everything's different. We're not the only industry that has been up-ended by the advent of social technologies and online commerce. So the idea that we can just plow ahead and continue to do what we've been doing is no longer true.

When companies are stagnating and there's a not a lot going on, they're told to "grow, grow, grow." But either they don't know how to do it or they've already tried and failed. This final part of the book will explore what can mature companies can do to reinvent themselves when growth is slowing.

What are the traps or risks of growing when you're already big? How can companies pick it up and regain momentum? What new approaches can companies embrace? What do you tell a company that's stale and stuck in the status quo? How do you enable them to grow?

Consider Shaklee, a company that was going to fade away if they didn't shake things up. If you look at them now, you'll notice that they've adapted to the new world by hiring a more modern thinking team and making other forward-looking changes. They've shifted from marketing to their traditional demographic and now focus on stay-at-home moms and a younger set, and trying to appeal to them in a new way. They're a good example of a formerly stale company that has reinvigorated itself.

You have to keep moving forward to maintain momentum, and I believe a company can do so if they continue to reinvent themselves."

Over and over, the CEOs and experts I interviewed emphasized the need for mature direct sellers to change what they do. As Kody Bateman says, "The key is to constantly reinvent yourself. Take a look at Apple computer. It's not even a computer company anymore; they now own 75% of global digital music sales and make a good portion of the world's smartphones. So that's a company that has dramatically reinvented itself over and over again. As a result, they're probably the premier technology company in the world today.

"There are many traditional ways that direct sales companies reinvent themselves, typically through new or different product lines or international expansion. You can never rest on your laurels. Right now I'm working on projects that are two to three years in the future. You have to keep moving forward to maintain momentum, and I believe a company can do so if they continue to reinvent themselves."

Richard Brooke is well aware of the need for mature companies to shake up the status quo. He recently announced that he would be moving his legendary company Oxyfresh out of the network marketing model altogether to concentrate on his much younger-focused nutritional brand LifeShotz.

"The older the organization, the more stagnant the management and the ideas. More people tend to hang on to what's working and don't want to shake things up. And I think you have to be willing to challenge the status quo, which at times includes your senior distributors and your top distributors. You have to be willing to irritate them and frustrate them, maybe even anger them, to keep fresh new ideas coming into the company."

For Ryan Wuerch, CEO of mobile services company Solavei, constant acceleration at all phases is a key factor in sustaining momentum. "Something that I've embraced for a very long time is that when the flywheel starts moving, continue to accelerate, continue to press on the gas. We're always focused on how we're continuing to propagate momentum within our network and take friction out of the system. We do it through technology and through creating more simplicity.

"I'll give you an example. Today, the enrollment process online or via mobile for a mobile phone, or all the other aspects of integration into Solavei, is night and day ahead of where it was a couple of years ago, just because technology continues to advance. So don't ever stop. We will never stop innovating; we'll never stop accelerating."

Let's look at some best practices for challenging old ways of doing business and bringing in the new.

When the flywheel starts moving, continue to accelerate, continue to press on the gas.

ORBIT LESSON #1

Battle the Culture of Boredom.

When a company is young, many direct sellers have a strong desire to build the business. But over time, as field leaders become more and more successful, they lose the initial drive they had to build their team. This can have a devastating effect on a mature company, as leaders move into maintenance mode, are reluctant to change, and prefer to maintain a status quo.

Complacency and an inability to reinvent themselves can make companies irrelevant. As one consultant tells me, "In the mid 1980s, there were a number of 'new' hybrid companies that managed to merge the high productivity from the party plan model with the high recruiting of the one-to-one model. These included Creative Memories, PartyLite, and Longaberger. All of them got to a very good size and were extremely successful, but over time they innovated less and less and were comparatively slow to adopt new technology. Perhaps they weren't eager to change the model that got them where they were. By failing to try bold new things, they hurt their growth."

For Richard Brooke, the question of fresh blood and fresh perspectives is of crucial importance.

> **The worst thing to happen strategically in a mature company is that the same people sitting around strategizing about how to create momentum are the same people that got you into no momentum.**

"If you haven't grown in five or 10 years, then culturally everybody in the company knows that. There's a systemic boredom and acceptance of 'we are who we are and we're not growing and there's nothing really exciting going on in our company.' And that attitude becomes the norm. It becomes the water to the fish. And if you try to stir that up with a lot of messages about change and a new vision, the challenge is that people don't tend to believe you. They don't pay attention because there's evidence around them, as well as historical evidence, that it's not going to happen.

Whereas a new company has the advantage of no history and no evidence. It's counter-intuitive, but people tend to believe a vision or a promise when there's no evidence to support it. So new companies are actually much more successful casting a vision of growth than a company that's been around for a while."

So how does an executive at a mature company address this?

Says Richard, "I would suggest that we all stand up, get out of our chairs, and get some fresh perspectives. Debate some of these strategies. The worst thing to happen strategically in a mature company is that the same people sitting around strategizing about how to create momentum are the same people that got you into no momentum. And it's not that the old wisdom isn't valuable. It's very valuable. But what's more valuable is getting some fresh blood in the room, which could be either younger executives with fresh perspectives, or even bringing in some new distributors. Find people who just joined the business in the last six months and ask them, 'Hey, what do you want out of this business? What inspired you? What kind of platform do you want to run on? What can we co-create together?'"

Kevin Larson, VP Sales and Field Development at New Earth, adds that it's certainly not lost on many leaders when they have stagnated and need to find new and interesting ways to attract new people. His advice is to work closely with those that are willing and remain engaged.

"Consider inviting them to initiatives the company is engaging to attract a younger crowd and show them the methodology you are using. When they are comfortable, challenge them and their budding young team to break old records. Although the habit will be for them to dive directly into teach the young ones 'how it's done'. This approach is not the one Millennials are looking for. Make it clear to them that the key to this initiative is to learn what they do not know, not simply teach what they do."

Although the habit will be for (older reps) to dive directly into teach the young ones 'how it's done'. Make it clear that the key is to learn what they do not know, not simply teach what they do.

ORBIT LESSON #2

Resist the Urge to Tinker.

In a mature company, when things are going well and sales are beginning to plateau, it can become an obsession of the company to make whatever changes are necessary to reverse the trend. It is a reasonable fear, as many companies have failed to react quickly enough to survive in this industry.

> If it is adopted and loved by all, keep it. If not, dump it.

As Kevin explains, "Before you do anything, consider this: your offering is new to your field every single day. For all those that are currently hearing the story, getting excited and engaged, things are new and fresh. They probably have no idea you are about to monkey with it!

"Before you make any changes, be deliberate about several things. First, study your data and know what the issues really are before you fix them. Second, create a win for every perceived negative change. Not a 'marketing spin' win, but a *real* legitimate win. Third, get buy-in and commitment from top leaders. Bring them along for the ride, (the field is less interested in surprises then you might think). Fourth, give yourself some room to save face. If you want to tinker with something in the compensation plan, first roll it out as a promotion for a time. If it is adopted and loved by all, keep it. If not, dump it."

ORBIT LESSON #3

Consider Shifts in Compensation to Increase Participation.

Then again, there are times when a big change is needed. I asked Richard to describe new ideas and methods that mature companies might use to rebuild momentum. He suggested innovative changes in compensation plans to create greater participation by the field and thereby reignite their enthusiasm.

"Historically, a network marketing or multilevel marketing company's compensation budget might be about 45% of revenue. If the company brings in a million dollars in a particular month, it's going to pay back to its sales force $450,000 in overrides. That same company might spend about 4% on events—a cruise contest, a national convention or some kind of an event where distributors get together.

"If you look at the compensation ratio, it's 90% cash, 10% some sort of an event. But whatever the event is, a distributor still has to pay her own travel expenses and take a loss of income from work to attend the events. In the future, I believe companies will shift that ratio. They'll pay less cash, because the difference between earning $800 a month and $900 a month is not significant. And once you get over $50,000 a month, does somebody really need to earn $100,000 or more a month? All of those 'ether level' incomes are wasted.

"So I see the ratio shifting, where instead of paying out so much in cash, companies might be looking to pay out less in cash and more in events. And what do they do with the extra money they're throwing into events? Pay all of the travel expenses for distributors. As a result, more people are likely to attend events, and you get more participation and 'high touch' in the culture. Companies will be eliminating the excuses for not getting together, which are always time and money."

ORBIT LESSON #4

Capture the Zeitgeist and Don't Let Go.

Another way for direct sales companies to maintain momentum in maturity is by tapping into new trends and markets. We are certainly living in a time where the collective spirit is changing.

For several years now I've spoken and written about GenY and Millennials and their impact on this industry, both present and future. It cannot be overstated. In *Social Selling* I discussed what the future may look like when Millennials take over, and laid out specific actions direct selling companies can take to connect with them, including changes to recognition programs, culture, comp planning, and of course social and mobile. Hopefully this is old news by now.

If your company has not taking seriously the tastes, motivations, psyches, preferences and habits of people under 35 years old (yes, they are that old now), you will soon be unpleasantly surprised to find that your recruiting slows to a crawl, your products are not in demand, and your attrition increases. A gradual decline will start to take hold. Maybe it already has.

When I speak about attracting Millennials, I don't mean just changing your marketing, creating new videos with lots of extreme sports, writing pithy copy, or re-skinning your website. These are just marketing band-aids. I'm talking about seeking to understand what makes you (or could make you) something Millennials would care about.

To achieve this, you may need to make fundamental changes in how you approach your business, in your marketing, products, team and mindset. You'll need to challenge long-held beliefs and "rules of thumb" in the industry and in your company.

The data is there. You know what Millennials want. The question you need to ask yourself is whether (or better, when) you can deliver it. As we've discussed, the need to stay in front of changes and culture shifts is critical.

For instance, we know that this generation craves connection. How are you enabling this, especially when they won't attend meetings or conference calls?

They crave technology. What kind of investments are you making in mobile and social?

They want adventure and new experiences. Are your incentive trips designed for this?

They want independence. Can your comp plan ultimately deliver it?

---

challenge long-held beliefs and "rules of thumb" in the industry and in your company.

The DSA recently cited a survey by the website Elance which reveals that only 35% of independent workers pursue additional work because of a need to earn extra income. Instead, people are looking for more job satisfaction and a more free lifestyle. In years past people expected to be in one career their entire lives. Now, as noted in the study, people have many careers over the course of a lifetime. Younger people, in particular, are more interested in non-traditional, non-linear work lives.

Now, more than ever, companies need to ask themselves whether they're doing all they can to match what they offer to the needs of the younger generation.

ORBIT LESSON #5

Keep Learning New Ways to Attract Younger Demographic.

How do you attract the younger generation? By looking for new patterns, themes and approaches. New companies have a lot to teach the veterans in our business about how to turn concepts Millennials relate to into successful direct selling companies.

One of the themes that really captivates Millennials is the desire to contribute to the social good. Noonday Collection of Austin, Texas, is a compelling new company that imports handmade jewelry from impoverished areas around the world that their "ambassadors" offer at trunk shows. Their story is one of transformation, not just of their field but the people who make their products. It's not self-improvement they preach, but *other* improvement.

This strikes a chord with people who seek to make an imprint on the world.

Another young company called Threads Worldwide is similarly focused on the social good. Like Noonday, they also sell products made by producers located in impoverished areas around the world.

I spoke with Threads co-founder Angela Yost about her company's focus on social responsibility.

"People aren't just out to make a buck anymore, and the idea of doing good with your purchases has become very popular.

"An example would be Tom's Shoes. They pioneered the idea that you can do good with the dollars that you spend. For every pair of shoes that you buy, they'll give a pair of shoes to kids around the world." Says Angela.

Indeed, many direct sellers have since mimicked this model and have begun their own buy and give programs.

Angela says direct selling makes more sense with the younger generation than ever before. "With people right out of college, direct selling doesn't have the baggage that it might have with older people. They just know, 'Oh, I could go and sell this stuff to my friends and make money while making a difference. And I get paid if one of my friends wants to do it with me? I'm in.' Direct sales is about community and networking, which are obviously so social, and people want be doing good at the same time and sell healthy and eco-friendly products. Why would younger people not want to do that?"

Direct sales is about community and networking, which are obviously so social, and people want be doing good things. Why would younger people not want to do that?

Another new company focused on younger consultants (possibly the youngest), is WillaGirl. With a strong focus on social media and technology, they are attempting to open a previously untapped market: Pre-teen girls and their moms. Founder Christy Prunier is laser-focused on reaching new markets and capitalizing on new trends because she knows she has to be knowledgeable about her market and meet them where they are.

"The girls are really driving the sales and are our most powerful ambassadors. They're looking for opportunities to earn money, and parents want their daughters to grow into confident self-starters. All this really lends itself well to direct selling."

ORBIT LESSON #6

Modernize Everything.

Keeping a company fresh and modern becomes increasingly difficult during the mature phase. Amway, one of the longest-operating direct sellers, has undertaken major initiatives to connect with younger audiences.

Andy Smith, General Manager of Amway UK, shared with me their initiatives to connect. "The biggest challenge we have is that the distributors who built the business in the 1970s and 80s aren't getting any younger," says Andy. "I've been a GM now for five years. Five years ago, the average age of our Leadership Group—about 100 leaders who have reached a certain level in the career plan—was about 55, because they built the business from the early days. How do we attract and be relevant to a younger population, and find new and younger leaders? How do we find a 25-year-old new distributor and take them through to leadership?

"Amway in Western Europe in the last two years has been conducting a modernization effort called the Renaissance Program, which consists of several key components.

"The digital support that we give to distributors has been really key in attracting the newer people. For example, up until a couple of years ago, we showed the business presentation on an old cardboard flipchart presenter or at best on PowerPoint slides. We since added an app called the Kiosk App, which you can show on a device--an iPad or an iPhone--with integrated videos and interactive connections to the website to show different products online. We've really worked hard on digital support to really connect with the younger generation.

"A second approach is finding new and relevant products for the younger generation. We've launched an energy drink recently in Europe called XS. It's more of a prospecting tool than a sales tool, to reach younger people who consume a lot of energy drinks. So that's been a big story for us, since the Amway distributor selling homecare and personal care products is seen as quite old-fashioned among the younger generation.

Everybody's nice and friendly, and there's the whole community spirit thing.

"The third idea, which has really taken off, is physical presence. Obviously, the business in the past has been done in the home, where the distributor goes to see a prospect, presents the opportunity, signs them up, gives them some products, and so on. Across Western Europe, we're now opening more and more Amway sales centers, which we call Experience Centers. We opened one in London five years ago, right in the heart of the city, and soon will have centers in Berlin and Rome. We have a retail area where distributors can show prospects and customers the product, and they can buy as well. There's a business lounge where they show prospects the business opportunity and sign them up on the premises. And then upstairs, the top floor is a meeting suite for our distributors and their teams.

"Now a distributor can bring a prospect into the center and they're not doing it cold. It's more of a demonstration than a sell. They just show people around and have them meet the rest of the team. Everybody's nice and friendly, and there's the whole community spirit thing. They sign people up easily because the distributors are confident about what they're talking about.

"The centers have really helped modernize the image of the company. It's helped us attract younger distributors for the first time in a long time."

Amway is a great example of a company in orbit that continually seeks out new worlds.

ORBIT LESSON #7

Mobile Is No Longer an Option. It's a Requirement.

The advent of mobile is a major boon for direct sellers. It's as if our industry asked the heavens for the perfect tool, and the gods granted it.

Mobile makes our mobile business *mobile*. It enables instant presentation, recognition, and connection wherever people are. It even leads to increases in production and retention.

Hopefully at this point any reader of this book understands the importance of offering first-rate mobile apps to their field. I discussed this in depth in *Social Selling* as well as in a white paper called *Action-packed Apps,* both of which described the impact of mobile on sales performance and productivity for direct sellers.

Mobile's really not an option anymore. The field demands a mobile solution for building their businesses. If you have even mild intentions of attracting a younger audience, you need a state-of-the-art mobile app that they would adopt.

Mobile app consultant Kate Donovan thinks direct selling tends to lag when it comes to technology. "It's proven out by the data," she says. "The average age of a distributor in the established companies in this industry is upwards of 55. While at the same time the 18 to 30 demographic in this industry has actually *declined* 13% from 2006-2013. That's because direct selling companies have not met them where they are — on mobile and social."

"Look at the web. It took a long time for the web to come into the direct selling industry. Ecommerce and online ordering, too. Then social media, same thing. But when we finally caught up, they transformed everything. The same thing is happening in mobile.

"Basically, if you want your company to thrive and grow, you have to be able to address Millennials. And the only thing that they understand is mobility."

It's as if our industry asked the heavens for the perfect tool, and the gods granted it.

Kate says the need for mobile is demonstrated by field behavior and preferences. "You have to be able to unchain people from their desks. The average distributor or consultant spends 6 hours or less per week working their business. That's about it. If they don't have a product in a mobile application that they could use to easily and quickly showcase and support their products on the go, they're not going to do the business."

Kevin Larson adds: "People want technology that is insanely simple. In every other consumer space that is exactly what they are receiving. I can edit videos, sign documents, click on what I like and skim what I don't, publish a book, and communicate in about 50 different ways all on my phone. And every one of these is just so simple to use. Apps have brought simplicity to some of the most complex tasks and they are only getting easier. Your distributors want and even expect the same that they get in the 'real' world."

ORBIT LESSON #8

Get Going on Mobile. Now.

Even with the perfect tool that the most coveted demographics are howling for, company adoption is still too slow. App consultant Kate Donovan estimates that fewer than 40% of industry companies are looking at mobility in a serious way. Others are poking around, kicking the tires, but mistakenly don't view it as critical. "Their plates are too full and so they just keep putting it off. But every day your company waits to build the app is a day the field isn't using it to sell."

One of the primary reasons it gets pushed out is the multiple people who are part of the decision. Certainly mobility is a significant decision, and it affects all departments in a company. Mobile is technology, so IT wants the plumbing a certain way. It's also a marketing tool, so Marketing wants the app to present well. The VP of Sales wants features that encourage selling. Training wants, well, training. And of course, the CFO wants the best deal. So who gets left out?

The field, because they end up with no app.

This is one of those times when the CEO needs to put a stake in the ground and insist on a world-class, field-centric app that contributes to the bottom line — with a firm deadline attached.

So, assuming you move forward with mobile, as you should, the question you should be asking now is *how will we implement it?* Will we choose a native app (the kind sold in the Apple or Android store) or a web app that works in the mobile browser? There are advantages and disadvantages to each.

First, let's consider whether you should build or buy. For larger organizations, it may make sense to leverage internal IT staff to develop your mobile app. This may be fine *if* they have the resources, the specialty skills required, *and* the time away from other projects to work solely on the app.

Although most IT staff will tell you they have the chops to build an app, it is really important to dig in and figure out if they can truly pull it off. Bottom line: You don't want to fail with an app, it's too high profile in the field.

My advice here would be to evaluate your internal team as if they were an outside vendor bidding on your app, without regard to cost. If they don't measure up, hire an outside specialty firm to build it, one that understands the industry and field behavior really well.

Kate Donovan outlined how mobile helps a direct seller:

"One of the best things is speed-to-sign up. You can enroll someone on the spot and they can be in business same day. Everything is right there. So they don't have to wait for their products to arrive—they can hold a virtual party that night. They don't have that lag time of waiting ten days for the package to arrive and all that buyer's remorse to set in."

Also, the business becomes much more duplicable. "With everyone on mobile, you have system dependency and that means that everybody is working from the same system so you're not dependent on your up-line to handhold you. You can choose to, but you don't necessarily have to. Because you don't need it."

How might mobile improve field communications?

Kate: "Mobile enables a company to provide one version of the truth to the field. Every time you make a change or want to notify the field, you can do so instantly. You can update their tools, marketing materials, notify them of promotions or inventory changes. Even the lawyers like having the ability to update old or erroneous documents that can be swapped out across the entire field, instantly.

"The training cycle of a mobile-enabled field is completely different because they're trained from a device that the home office controls. Everyone is singing from the same hymnal. Again, that's system dependency."

So what is the most important consideration in building your app? *Adoption.*

Adoption is the quintessential measure of the success of your app. If you don't have it, not only have you wasted all the time, effort, and resources poured into the app, you'll have cost yourself in credibility with the field as well. Whatever path you choose, the field must love your app.

Whatever path you choose,
the field must love your app.

ORBIT LESSON #9

Examine your Communication.

The times have certainly changed, and the way things are effectively communicated have changed with them. One way we can modernize is by changing the way we communicate with prospects and the general public.

Andy Smith of Amway: "We've been using the same language to the talk to the public as we did 40 years ago, words that people don't really understand anymore.

"We've worked with communication experts and conducted focus groups to determine how the general public reacts to a distributor's presentation.

"We looked at the communication word-by-word, and now we know that our words work differently for a female prospect, a male prospect, or a younger prospect. So we've really refined the things we say to prospects to make it more relevant, because we can be a little mysterious in the ways we describe things. Even some of the older leaders and distributors are using this new terminology and getting good results from it.

"Here's a quick example. We've been using the word 'dream' forever at Amway, which is probably common throughout the industry. You say to a prospect, 'What's your dream?' You talk about the big car, the fantasy boats, and the big houses. But in reality, that doesn't connect these days. They don't want to be a millionaire in five years; they want to earn $200 this month. So instead of using the word 'dream,' we're using the word 'imagine.'—imagine getting $200 a month to pay for your kid's school trip or a nifty holiday. We're getting some really great reaction to that, and we're measuring the response from prospects who get that new, updated message.

"The research has also helped us change the way we hold meetings. Our leaders always wore a three-piece suit and tie. A guy would typically present the business model, with his wife in the background maybe doing a product display and not saying anything. This scored poorly with the younger generation. Basically, people saw us as too corporate. The research shows that the general public trusts female speakers more than males in pitching the sales. So we've had male and female partners sharing equal time in the presentations. And they've stopped wearing suits and ties. They're more connected and more relaxed. The research has been really illuminating in helping us connect."

Talk about the big car, the fantasy boats, and the big houses doesn't really connect these days.

ORBIT LESSON #10

Take a Closer Look at Your Bonuses.

We mentioned earlier the success at several companies of "Three and Free" programs that have since led to a rush for many other companies to jump on the bandwagon and offer their own. As usual, there may be a few gotchas. In addition to the legal issues that Spencer Reese mentioned in Part 1 of this book, there may be practical reasons to reconsider it.

Kevin Larson at New Earth believes it is counterproductive. "First, it sets up an expectation that the product is worth it to me…when it's free. Suppose in a certain month one of my 'three' falls through and doesn't purchase. Now I have to pay for the product I expected to receive gratis. In my frustration, maybe I decide I will not purchase either now that I am forced to. Now the guy above me has a problem, right?

"These things eat themselves from the bottom up simply because people begin to expect something for free forever. In a 'relationship and trust' business, free is a lousy reward, as it goads what could otherwise be preferred customers into joining for a promise—which rarely happens, and depends on treating other people as a means to an end. My primary issue is simply this, 'free' is not always the best word to describe products of high quality and caliber. It may prompt a customer to ask, 'well how good could it really be?' I love the free samples at Costco, but I would think twice if they were dumping boxes in my cart."

Another long-standing method the industry uses to reward people who achieve a new rank up is to give them a "car bonus." Car programs have long been an important driver (sorry) of growth for many companies. It is sometimes the single biggest motivator in a comp plan.

The car is typically in the company's name and the company covers the lease costs. It doesn't cost the company anything—rather than pay cash, they pick up the car payments. This obviously can serve as good marketing for the company if consultants are driving around in a new Mercedes. People take notice and it piques interest. Happy rep, happy company, right?

Maybe for a little while. The problem with these bonuses is that, because they are so exciting to reps, companies over time tend to lower the bar for qualification requirements, and that gets a lot of everyday people into trouble.

Let's say Joe is a recipient of a new car, but soon enough he falls down in rank and is forced to pick up the payments. If Joe leaves the company, he may not be able to carry the lease, which can go against him on his credit. Worse, if he can't make the payments, the car can be (and often is) repossessed.

How does that look to Joe's family and neighbors? Absolutely awful. You can just imagine his friends and family, many of whom incidentally Joe would have previously approached about joining the company): "Joe failed at that business, just like I told him he would. What a sham."

A loss for Joe, no doubt. But also for the company. And the industry.

This will probably stir some debate, but my opinion is the car bonus, unless safeguarded, is highly detrimental to not only the people who "earn" them but to the industry as a whole. People who make money in this business should be educated in managing it responsibly, rather than encouraged to buy more car than they can afford.

Yes, it is exciting for a rep to be able to win something as cool as a new car in return for their hard work. And yes, having thousands of people driving around in a new exotic automobile is great marketing for the company.

But the car bonus is a deleterious influence on the business and we should award them differently. Either reps actually *earn* a car (rather than the right to drive a leased car until a rough patch), or we figure out a more sustainable, authentic and honest reward.

The problem with car bonuses is that, because they are so exciting to reps, companies over time tend to lower the bar for qualification requirements, and that gets a lot of everyday people into trouble.

ORBIT LESSON #11

Get to the Next Level, Even When You're Already at the Top.

A challenge for many mature companies is reaching the next level in growth. For example, only a handful of direct sellers have reached $1 billion in revenue. What distinguishes those companies in our industry that reach certain milestones of performance? The leaders? The company culture? The products? The markets they focus on?

Terrell Transtrum mentions the power of adding fresh executive leadership to re-ignite momentum.

"I ran into Orville Thompson, CEO of Scentsy, last June at the DSA annual meeting. And I said: 'Orville, what keeps you up at night?' He rolled his eyes and said 'You know what, we're stuck at our current level of revenues. And I have yet to figure out how to fire it up further. That's what I've never solved. How do we get from where we are to that next level?

"He acknowledged slower growth and the issue of needing to recreate momentum. And the principles that we're talking about here are applicable not only to the launch stage, but even at a huge successful company like Scentsy.

One reason for slower growth at more mature companies is the tenure of the field. As Jamie Stewart, former DSA UK chairman and Managing Director of Momentum Factor's European offices, points out, "When the company is young, many direct sellers have a strong desire to build the business. Over time, as the leaders are more and more successful they reap the benefits in terms of income, and as a result can lose the initial drive they had. This can have devastating effects on the business, as the leaders move into maintenance mode, are reluctant to change, and prefer to maintain a status quo."

Another reason for stalled growth is the natural tendency for the field to go off on their own directions. Jamie Stewart: "As multi-level organizations mature, fragmentation is also a common problem. Communication breaks down with the field, teams deteriorate as people have conflicts, or leaders leave and leave behind orphaned teams. A solid corporate communications program to build and unite the team behind the mission of the company can combat the impact of this."

Perhaps this is the result of a "retirement-oriented" comp plan that rewards longevity over performance, or maybe an ageing of the field who grow into different priorities and simply lose interest over time, the good news about both of these is they can be managed through innovation in compensation, communications and marketing.

You are perfectly aligned to get the results that you're getting... you need to disrupt that alignment in order to fuel new momentum.

Terrell Transtrum: "Steven Covey said 'You are perfectly aligned to get the results that you're getting.' In other words, everything that's going on in your company today is perfectly situated to get you exactly the results that you're getting. And you have to disrupt that alignment in order to fuel new momentum.

ORBIT LESSON #12

What Got You Here May Not Get You There.

Strong and adaptive leadership is key is in helping mature companies reinvent themselves and continue to grow.

Terrell Transtrum emphasizes the need to ensure you have the right management for the stage you're at. "As companies grow, needs change. Mary Kay Ash took her company to a certain level, and then her son took it to the next. Later, an executive named Dick Bartlett came on board. While aligned with the purpose and mission of the company, he brought fresh strategies and perspectives to propel the company to an even higher level.

"The same thing happened with Amway. Dick DeVos and Jay Van Andel took Amway to a certain point, then their sons stepped in at the right time and, to their own credit, took it to an entirely new level. They did an amazing job of bringing new momentum via new leadership. Same situation at Avon. So that's a common thread."

"Herbalife, when Mark Hughes ran it, would be another good example," says Terrell. "The company was very much driven and influenced by his personality, to the point that it was in a state of limbo for some time when he died, until Michael Johnson took over. What Michael has done since is to focus on team, not individual personality, with great effect."

"Herbalife is a great example of a company reinventing itself, first by adding corporate know-how to the senior team through Johnson's leadership, then by repositioning its marketing and embracing technology well in all of its markets. The combination has resulted in Herbalife enjoying a sustained period of growth."

Jamie Stewart of Momentum Factor (Europe) also emphasizes the need for simplicity in more established companies. "Over time, mature businesses can become very complex as new features or initiatives are introduced to address a particular issue. In contrast, new companies are often simple and easy to understand. Companies should take time to think about what it's like from a new starter perspective or new customer perspective."

Sheila Marcello, VP Marketing at ACN, Inc., says her company is focused on adapting to constantly changing needs of their field. "Like everything else, our business building and support systems have changed and evolved over the years, right along with technology. This means changing and adapting to ensure we are meeting our target market head on, in a place that is comfortable for them.

"For example, we've grown just fine through the years without the use of a social media platforms. It simply wasn't a requirement in the past. But we know that we won't continue to grow as a company without social media, so it has become a mainstay of our communication platform."

Case Study: NuSkin: Results Demonstrated.

Dan Jensen describes NuSkin as an example of a company that reinvented itself in the mature phase.

"NuSkin is approaching its thirtieth year in business and $2.5 billion in revenue. In the last five to eight years, they have been involved in extensive efforts to strengthen their story. Their tagline is 'NuSkin: Results Demonstrated.' Those last two words are new. And it correlates with the double-digit growth curve they're experiencing today, not a common thing in mature companies. Usually it's stable or declining. They have some markets that are growing massively. Their domestic market is growing significantly. A good part of it is due to the re-establishment of their story.

One part of that story is that they have designed their products to be more personal. "They're teaching their sales force to utilize technology to establish each client's specific nutritional needs. Pharmanex, their nutritional line, allows for a personalized nutritional program. After three months of using the product, your distributor comes back and takes another measure. Clearly, as a result of nutritional supplements, your measures are going to be better. As a result, retention rates on auto-ship are higher, customer loyalty is higher, and distributor volumes are higher. It's because the company can demonstrate results, something difficult to do with supplements.

NuSkin discovered this years after its launch, but this is a perfect example of how a company can re-launch and differentiate itself.

Jamie Stewart, former DSA UK Chair and leader of Momentum Factor's European offices, points to Herbalife as another good example of a successful relaunch. "Herbalife is also experiencing double-digit growth. Some years ago they changed their approach to focus on nutrition centers, which a Herbalife distributor sets up in their home or a small storefront. People visit the center on the way to work and buy a diet shake from you. In Mexico, Herbalife has 27,000 nutrition centers. And half or more of the company's sales come from those centers, not distributors' personal consumption. This new business model has enabled them to reinvent themselves."

ORBIT LESSON #13

Be Alert For New Approaches to the Model.

I asked Bart Dangerfield of RBC Life about his company longevity and what they might be learning from new entrants. He said their long tenure is both a help and a hindrance.

"We've taken a good solid look at our existing field and who we're attracting. We know of that by doing what we've always done will continue to get what we've got. We've got an older demographic, not that edgy, and generally a product user. Even our younger associates who've signed up have done so really because they just want the product.

"So we've watched new companies coming out and looked at what they're doing, and we need to be honest with ourselves and say, you know what, we love customers. We love 'em.

"The old paradigm was sign anybody up as distributor even if they're customers and hopefully you'll be able to convert them just by calling them a distributor. Our plan is to make that distinction clear upfront just so you know someone's preference coming in and treat them accordingly. The newer companies are doing that from the outset, drawing a distinct separation between customer and field."

I spoke with Ryan Wuerch, CEO at Solavei, about his company's effort to create an economic linkage between mobile service, social commerce, and social networking technology. This linkage seems to be an indicator of the new landscape we're in, and I asked Ryan to talk about its importance to his company and the industry as a whole.

"We looked at what Costco does to make commerce less expensive yet profitable," Ryan says. "They have millions of members and use their collective buying power as leverage to drive down the price of property, goods, and services, and pass those savings on to the members. We're doing the same thing, except we're not using a brick and mortar warehouse; we're using social media and a social network platform that enables individuals to do this all through technology.

Our plan is to make that distinction clear upfront just so you know someone's preference coming in and treat them accordingly.

"Part of our platform enables our members to connect into community. The tagline of our company is 'powered by relationships.' The people who have become members of Solavei have gotten here because of someone else forwarding them a link. They clicked on a graphic or they clicked on a tweet, and then enrolled with us for mobile service."

I asked Ryan if he felt the industry was up to speed in using new approaches.

"Companies in the direct sales industry tend to use social media as somewhat of a plug-in, maybe they have a Facebook page or Twitter account. We actually designed our company to serve *as* social commerce network. We have built it that way from day one. Traditional direct sellers will get a product and some distributors, create a comp plan, and put technologies in place to facilitate the movement of products through the distribution channel. But in the future you'll see an entirely different model—more companies creating themselves purely as technology and social network companies.

"We've built our platform not based on a domestic market but on a global social exchange. Our objective is, every time there's something new that can benefit the customer, we're pushing it right to them. We want to create a one-to-one relationship with them, no different than the relationship I have with Amazon today. It might have been a friend of mine that referred me to Amazon. In the same way, the person who enrolls me into Solavei gets the benefit."

When I asked Rob Snyder of Stream Energy about particular strategies or approaches he was considering to reinvent; he also seemed to be thinking about social commerce on an Amazon/retail services scale.

"When you get into the mature phase, it can become difficult to reinvent yourself. We're actually in the process of reinventing Stream and Ignite (Stream's network marketing arm) due to the the intensification of competition in the energy markets over the last 10 years. The reason that we originally chose electricity as our first product was, number one, because of the opportunity presented by energy deregulation, and second, because people were already buying energy and electricity.

"We believe a web-driven consumer environment will develop where direct sellers can create downlines of customers who will be self-selecting and self-bundling, in the same way that Comcast, AT&T, and other firms are already trying. You provide a very inviting online environment for consumers that's driven by a vanguard of direct sellers, with all of these services being sold under a single brand name, whether they're like-labeled or not, with consumers being rewarded for self-bundling. And if this entire platform is linked to social networks, consumers will be able to share their savings experiences.

"That's actually how we're trying to innovate and reinvent ourselves right now, because we are in a decidedly mature phase as an energy retailer."

ORBIT LESSON #14

Think Globally, Act Globally.

In addition to expanding services and product lines, many companies continue to look abroad for growth. There are mature companies in the U.S., tweaking and refining, who float around in the orbit stage. But mature companies across the globe are rocketing. International expansion is currently a major industry growth area.

Companies are moving into Korea, Japan, Eastern Europe, China, Africa, and many developing countries, riding a wave of entrepreneurialism that crosses all borders and geographies. There's a hunger in developing countries for entrepreneurship and the ability to master one's own economic destiny, and social media and mobile technologies are making it possible.

This is what our model appeals to—the ability to develop yourself personally and professionally, to build an income that you couldn't have had before, to be an entrepreneur and learn how to run a business without an advanced education. All those things are a powerful part of what we offer to the world.

Some are actually built to develop other countries. BHIP Global of Dallas uses an opportunistic strategy of "going where the teams are." They'll find a leader in a country and support that leader, whether in Thailand, New Guinea, Korea, or wherever. Their focus is to figure out the customs of the country and how to build there, and then they go for it. They don't go into a country and hope they find people to build; they find the leaders and build from there. And it works.

Andy Smith of Amway is well aware of the opportunities and challenges that mature companies face in international markets.

Amway is one of the most well-established companies in existence. How can they further develop at their mature stage? Andy explains: "We've pretty much expanded into every market we can. A third of our business comes out of Asia, and that's a fairly new market. Of our total global sales of $12 billion, 30% comes from China. For other companies China's a new territory, but for us it's a middle-aged, not quite mature market. We're in 80 countries worldwide, pretty much everywhere you can be.

"So having penetrated most of the markets, the question we're working on now is how do we provide better service and access to the distributor within all the markets? One of our strategies is to support different community groups in our various markets.

"For example, in the UK, particularly in London, there's a huge cultural mix, people from Africa, Latin America, Thailand, and China. We offer different website versions for all those languages—just in the UK alone. If you're Spanish and live in the UK and you click on the Spanish flag, you can do your business in Spanish with Amway here.

"We have product trainers in the field who conduct training in Russian, Spanish, Thai, Chinese. We have simultaneous translation at all our big conferences. The fastest growing population for Amway in Germany is the Turkish-speaking group, so we provide them with distributor tools in their own language. By giving people the support they need, we're trying to strengthen our existing markets."

ORBIT LESSON #15

A New Market Can Change Who You are, If You Let It.

Kevin Young of RBC Life leads a hectic international schedule. I asked him what the challenges are for growing a mature company internationally.

"I think a major challenge companies face is integrating their domestic culture into international markets. The way you sync, the way you behave, the way that you interact with the customers or distributors is substantially different internationally. Understanding the local culture first and foremost is more important than anything else. To do that you need to find somebody that is local to that culture or community that can take your message, your brand, your company, and integrate it into the local market.

I asked Kevin how going international can change a company operationally.

"The first thing we do is find someone local who has been on our side of the business who understands the legalities and traps in moving products into the market. For instance, when we opened Taiwan, we had a consultant who knew right away which ingredients in our products would not work. We had to make a decision. Do we change the formulation for the market? Or do we reduce the number of SKUs or products that we provide to the market?

"And as a company, we made the decision that we would not change the ingredient of the product and chose not to enter that product into the market. So we have a smaller footprint there. In countries abroad we generally we have smaller line of products and fewer SKUs. In Hong Kong or in Taiwan, we have 10; where domestically we have 40 or so."

So the lesson here is at some point you may be forced to choose whether to compromise your product or values, or not enter a new market.

"If you have something that's a core competency and you want to bring your core competency or value proposition to a new market but the regulations won't allow it, then you really don't have anything to bring to that market. So if we can't sell our proprietary products in a country, it's not of interest to us to build a business there. It just doesn't make any sense, because we build our entire story around those core products."

ORBIT LESSON #16

Every Country Is a Snowflake.

How is direct selling different abroad than at home?

Kevin Young: "The direct selling methodology is different in every single country. For instance, the dependence on recruiting is often much higher internationally than domestically. Here, we train people and create customers out of them. People buy the product and then tell the story.

"Internationally, especially in Asia, they bring people in to make money. So you really need to understand what the metrics are going to look like when you start bringing people in. How do you move them from initial purchase to finding value in a monthly autoship over and over again and becoming a customer? A lot of us in this industry overlook the value of autoship internationally.

"I think that's a real big trap. You can load a lot of people in, but if they don't stay, you really accomplish nothing. All you've done is moved an initial order and then every single month you're in recruiting mode rather than building them as storytelling customers and building volume that way."

Successful models vary across borders as well. Rayner Urdaneta, Managing Director of L'Eudine Global, a successful health and beauty company with markets in South America, uses variations of the model in different countries. In Colombia, they use a product pre-pack model where they ship forty products to the consultant completely on credit terms. In order to encourage on-time payments, they give away prizes like small appliances, flat screens and smartphones. Once the pack is all sold, the distributor re-orders.

Mexico however is a different model. Says Rayner, "In Mexico where minimum wage is one of the lowest in Latin America, the forty products pack is perceived as too expensive. So, the company had to change the model closer to the network marketing with the used of replicated websites and virtual stores taking away the need to order a product pack.

The fields behave very differently across countries as well. "Virtually all the biggest direct sales companies have a presence in Mexico, and sales force will hop to another company if they don't feel they are getting flexibility. So, the company had to change the model closer to the network marketing with the used of replicated websites and virtual stores taking away the need to order a 40 product pack.

Rayner emphasized the importance of customizing to every geography. "With the great success we had in Venezuela with our unique direct sales model, we assumed that we would just easily replicate the success in other Latin American countries if we simply exported our best leaders.

"We learned the hard way for example that even though Mexico is part of Latin America with the same language, this North American country is a more competitive market with major cultural differences from a South American country like Venezuela. I would always advise not to treat geographical blocks with the same strategy. Not just for cultural reason but because differnet countries accept different sales models.not all the countries accept the same direct sales models.

ORBIT LESSON #17

Structure Each Country's Program around the Economic Realities of That Country.

Kevin Young at RBC Life, says, "In Mexico or even in some of the third-world countries, where business is starting to really grow, it's still a cash business. What we discovered was we could not mandate that our 70 dollar product be purchased all at once. It could be an aggregate 10 seven dollar orders, or seven 10 dollar orders. This was a big lesson learned, because here in the US a $70 price point is not unreasonable.

"When you start to transfer that over to an international market, for example, Taiwan, our starter kit is the equivalent of about a week's income for individuals. You really need to think creatively to meet their economic needs. If we burden people upfront in these markets, they can't play.

"We're looking at the Philippines and Vietnam sometime next year, both very poor countries. How do you ask people there to purchase five-hundred dollars' worth of products just to get started? It takes really thinking through the compensation, local economies, and behaviors, almost from scratch, each time."

ORBIT LESSON #18

Commit to Making the Industry Better.

If you're on top of the industry press then probably already know, there are forces at work to try and tear this business apart. Part of it is companies' own doing. They might ignore their field's salesforce raids and proselytizing. Or pull distributorships when the checks get too high. Or throw up their hands while their reputations are smeared, only to let it fester, or allow distributors to run amok with false claims, for fear of rocking the boat.

But many of these forces are outside our control. Short-sellers on Wall Street engaged in cynical money grabs, regulators who don't really understand us., and politicians seeking a name for themselves.

These are big, important and industry-defining challenges.

The importance of a unified industry cannot be overstated. The challenges are just too great for any company to think they are immune. Party plan or person-to-person, high tech or traditional, if your company pays its reps in multiple levels of commission, you are subject to all these risks, and it is incumbent upon companies to do everything they can to safeguard the future.

Fortunately we have a trade association whose staff wakes up every day and goes to work to protect our industry's interests. The Direct Selling Association and its foundation, the Direct Selling Education Foundation, champion our industry by educating lawmakers and the public on the benefits of the model, and its members on ethics, integrity, and best practices.

Needless to say, recently they have been particularly busy as of late, working diligently on behalf of all of us. The DSA's swift response to the recent short seller attacks were nothing short of outstanding.

I truly believe that our firm and our clients would not be able to operate in our current fashion if not for the efforts of this great organization. I recommend companies get involved, join the committees, attend the events and contribute time and money.

We owe a lot of our success to the DSA.

ORBIT LESSON #19

Become a Futurist.

One of my passions is futurism, especially as it pertains to business. I am always interested in where things might go, both expected and unexpected routes. How decisions made today or how opportunities seized or missed can shape our future world, and that to me is fascinating.

Apple, for instance, has shaped our world, of that there is no doubt. But to study their history you would know that they had several near misses that nearly put them out of business. Bill Gates even bailed them out at a low point. If they had disappeared, our world might look very different today. At least our gadgets would.

For us to be successful in this business, we all need to study the future and what may come. Changes in demographics, technology, management, operations, marketing, the whole lot. We need to be able to see around corners and be ready to adapt.

I asked our experts to give a picture of what the future of the industry might look like. Several spoke about how the industry is finally shedding its negative baggage, especially among Millennials, and that means Millennials are not only a great focus from a short term point of view, but they represent the biggest opportunity we have.

"Although there is still somewhat of a stigma about who we are and what we do," Richard Brooke says, "that stigma is loosening up some, especially among younger people. I've taken a video camera and a film crew, and hit the streets and just interviewed people. I ask them: 'What do you know about network marketing and multi-level marketing? What do you know about direct sales? What companies come to mind when I say those things?'

"I was amazed at the responses that I got. With older people, the stigma's still in place. But younger people don't know what direct selling is and don't have the negative connotations. What's changing to our advantage is that the demographic is changing. The younger generation does not have a negative attitude about what we do. So educating people about the business is an important consideration."

Kimberly Cornwell agrees. Not only does direct selling have a more positive image with the younger generation, she says, but that generation is much more

entrepreneurial by nature.

"I think the future's great for direct selling. Younger people are not aware of some of the old business practices back in the day and I think the stigma is gone.

"In addition, the ideal job for people in their 20s and 30s is not to be sitting in a cubicle in corporate America. Their ideal is to have everything. They want to be entrepreneurs. They want their own time. They want social responsibility. And they want to have fun as they learn and grow. Direct sales offers that."

Christy Prunier of WillaGirl says people need to be educated on how valuable the industry is, not only for self-expression but also personal growth.

> In addition, the ideal job for people in their 20s and 30s is not to be sitting in a cubicle in corporate America. Their ideal is to have everything. They want to be entrepreneurs. They want their own time. They want social responsibility. And they want to have fun as they learn and grow. Direct sales offers that.

"As I look at the behavior of girls over the last 10 years, there's been 30% less traffic to the malls. They're not going to the malls anymore. The way they're socializing is very much in the home and online with peers. This trend is tailor-made for the direct selling industry. So the greater challenge is keeping up with these 'digital natives'—young people who are savvy and deft with technology. We need to make sure that the innovation is there that makes it as experiential as possible. Those are areas where I'd be excited to see the industry gain traction."

Kody Bateman of SendOut Cards cites the eternal need for people to make extra money as a bright spot for direct selling.

"In the future, two factors are going to influence the momentum of the industry. The first is social media and the second is economic trends that we'll see over the next 10 years. Lots of top economists believe we are going to be in a state of recession, not only in North America, but also pretty much throughout the world, which is bad news for the world but not so bad for direct sales. People do need a Plan B, as it's going to be a challenge to earn a living in traditional ways. So I think we're going to see major growth in direct sales over the next 10 years, as people learn more about it through social media and continue to need an alternative income. It's a really exciting time to be in this profession."

As I researched this book, compiled notes and conducted interviews, there were a few stand out themes. First, the long view for our industry is one of optimism, as Kody alludes to. The experts and leaders I spoke with express a wide range of views about building and sustaining momentum in direct selling. They may not all agree on what works best or even what the future of the model will be. But they are all in agreement: the revolutionary changes taking place now are actually *good* for our industry.

Social media? Made for us. Smartphones in every pocket? The perfect selling tool. Mainstream competition? Helps keep us focused on what makes us special. Even increased regulatory scrutiny will push us to better practices and sort out the money games that give us a black eye.

The trends are in our favor.

Second, a deep faith in the core values and principles of our industry provides guidance to the leading companies whether they are in the launch phase, accelerating, or in orbit. There's an abiding belief that direct selling's products and business model fulfill the needs people have had in the past, the present, and likely the future: human connections and sharing, freedom and independence, and healthy products, environmentally and socially conscious and fun to use.

Finally, the acknowledgement that the old ways of doing business are no longer sufficient signifies that our industry is ready for the next mission. Everyone with whom I spoke expressed the need to adapt to and embrace change—technological change, economic change, and cultural change.

We can only do so if we meet people where they are—where they communicate and hang out, with products that truly help them lead better lives, and with opportunities that can help them fulfill themselves in ways that go beyond money.

My hope is that the wisdom presented in this book by some of the smartest people I know will help you find new ways to become the best at what you do and to always keep moving forward.

ABOUT THE AUTHOR

Jonathan Gilliam is a highly-regarded expert in areas of social media, marketing, reputation management and compliance monitoring, dedicated to serving direct selling companies. He is the author of *Social Selling: How Direct Selling Companies Can Harness the Power of Connectivity—and Change the World*, a widely-read industry-focused book on social media.

Jonathan is Founder and President of Momentum Factor, the leading international social media and online marketing management firm specializing in the direct selling industry.

Prior to establishing the firm, he was the co-founder and former Chief Marketing Officer of a successful direct selling company and served as a Senior Marketing Executive with another major direct seller.

Jonathan has an extensive background in Internet technology and interactive marketing. He was Co-Founder & CEO of Hush Communications, a successful Internet software company in Dublin, Ireland; Marketing Strategy Partner at a national management consulting firm OneAccord; served global consultancy Deloitte as a Senior Manager in Marketing and Business Development, and worked at an AdAge Top 50 interactive firm as Account Director.

Jonathan is an accomplished speaker and presenter on industry topics and has He is a regular presenter at Direct Selling Association conferences, is a co-founder of the Direct Selling

Symposium and creator and co-founder of the Direct Selling CXO Summit. He has appeared in numerous international radio and television broadcasts, articles and conferences including the New York Times, Wired Magazine, The Wall Street Journal, Associated Press, PC Week, National Public Radio, and multiple appearances on TechTV's "Silicon Spin" with John Dvorak, among others.

Jonathan graduated with a BA degree from the University of Texas at Austin (*Hook 'Em!*) followed by graduate studies at Rice University in marketing and publishing.

He resides in Austin, Texas with his wife and three daughters.

Have Jonathan speak at your next event.

Jonathan's captivating presentation will inspire your field in the areas of Social Selling and train them how to do it right so everyone wins. His speaking style is fun, humor laden, energetic, and personal. For speaking references send him an email at Jonathan@MomoFactor.com about speaking at your next meeting or convention.

Join Us at:
www.facebook.com/momentumfactor
www.twitter.com/momofactor
www.linkedin.com/in/jonathangilliam
www.youtube.com/momofactor
www.MomoFactor.com

Subscribe to the MomoNews newsletter for industry executives at our website!

ABOUT MOMENTUM FACTOR

Our mission is to provide best-in-class marketing & management services to the world's finest direct selling companies and field leaders. Our firm works to maximize performance for clients by increasing revenue, protecting brands, engaging field & customers, and multiplying Momentum. Most of all, our aim is to become high-value, indispensible partners with our clients for the long term.

"In my opinion, values are more than simple statements like 'we have integrity' or 'we put our client first.' Our values represent powerful ideas about who we are as a firm and how we make decisions under uncertainty or duress, and importantly,what we would give up if we had to make a choice." ~ Jonathan Gilliam

Impactful and Effective Online Services for Direct Sellers

Social Media Excellence Program
- Full Managed Social Media
- Startup and Fast Growth & Established Company Programs
- Social Media Training for the Field
- Online Marketing and Lead Generation
- Direct Sales Video, Multimedia and Creative Services

Online Risk Mitigation Services
- Reputation Defense
    - o Fully Managed Reputation Management Services
- FieldWatch Online Compliance Monitoring Service
    - o Monitoring Technology plus Compliance Management and Enforcement

Marketing Service Exclusively for Direct Sellers
- Strategic Marketing
- Complete Corporate Email & Field Communications

Outsourcing
- Startup, Launch and Growth Marketing Consulting
- Automated Compliance Monitoring
- Online Reputation Repair & Protection
- World-class Marketing Strategies

"We develop 'best-in-class'programs for our clients and manage them on an ongoing basis. Rather then drop off a report, or a training session, or 'strategy,' we work with our clients to build their platforms, and their culture, to respect and leverage the power of Social Selling to not only build their following but bring a return on their investment."

CORE VALUES

1. We believe that we're here to make a difference by helping the companies who help people.

2. We choose to work with clients where we can make a significant contribution.

3. We believe in simplicity versus complexity, clarity over obtuseness.

4. We covet only projects that are truly important and meaningful to our clients and us.

5. We believe in collaboration with our clients and partners, driving quality and innovation.

6. We don't settle for anything less than honesty, integrity and excellence.

7. We value family, friendship, community and spirit.

Please contact us if we can be of service!

Momentum Factor
4412 Spicewood Springs Rd. Suite 201
Austin, Texas 78759
+1 512.994.4646
jonathan@momofactor.com
www.MomoFactor.com